New Hampshire
War and Peace

John Clayton

PETER E. RANDALL PUBLISHER
Portsmouth, New Hampshire
2001

ISBN 0-9650684-4-7

These articles first appeared in the Union Leader and are used in revised
form with permission of the Union Leader Corporation

Bob LaPree's cover photo of the author was taken before the Spanish-
American War Memorial in Manchester's Bronstein Park

Produced by Peter E. Randall Publisher
P.O. Box 4726
Portsmouth, NH 03802

Additional copies available from
John Clayton
241 North Street
Manchester, NH 03104

To Seaman First Class Robert N. Clayton, Sr.

*Landing Signal Officer aboard the USS Casablanca
who made certain his six children touched down safely
on the deck of life*

Contents

Acknowledgments

NEW HAMPSHIRE has a rich military history. It is a history shaped by individual stories. Those stories speak to courage and sacrifice and love of country. Still other stories speak to an abiding love and respect for those who serve.

This is but a small sampling of those stories.

Rather than a comprehensive, chronological work, I have chosen to present New Hampshire's military stories the way they come to me. They come to me randomly. They come to me in an episodic fashion, and those episodes, when viewed collectively, reflect a whole that is greater than the sum of its parts.

Many people have helped make this book possible. I am, as always, deeply indebted to my wife Colleen, my daughter Jennifer and the others who make up my remarkable family. In particular, in this instance, there is my father, Bob Sr., and my two big brothers, Tom and Bob Jr., who wore the uniform of the United States Navy.

I also extend thanks to my colleagues at *The Union Leader*. There is Publisher Joe McQuaid, who offers encouragement and unparalleled latitude. There is Managing Editor Pat Sheeran, who helps me make sense of all that computer stuff. There is Veterans Page Editor Greg Andruskevich, who gives me first dibs on the many moving stories that come his way, and then there is my good friend, photographer and collaborator Bob LaPree who, like me, believes in the importance of sharing these stories. His talents are exceeded only by the passion he brings to his work.

Lastly, I could not do this without the people who have shared their tales with me. I thank the many veterans, their friends and their loved ones, who have chosen to trust me with stories so warm and human and moving and sacred.

For more than 50 years, Bert Smith's family knew little more about his death than they did when they first received word of his disappearance in 1944. (Union Leader Photo Illustration by Tom Lynch)

Missing...

FOR 56 YEARS, Marine Corps Sgt. Bertrand L. Smith was lost. Now he's found.

It is a tale of amazing grace. Through the unflagging persistence of a friend and fellow Marine and the diligence of a scientist billed as "the Indiana Jones of military archaeology," the wreckage of the plane that carried Bert Smith to his death on Nov. 10, 1944 has been discovered in the Western Pacific.

The final resting place for the Manchester man and his two Marine colleagues is a dense mangrove swamp on the coral atoll that is Peleliu Island. It was there where their torpedo bomber—a TMB-1C Avenger—went down shortly after take-off.

That it was lost for more than half a century is a mystery, the kind of mystery a former Marine named John Lally could not abide. The kind that Dr. Patrick Scannon and colleagues like Chip Lambert like to solve.

For the past seven years, Scannon—the chief science and medical officer for Xoma, a pharmaceutical technology firm in northern California—has been visiting remote islands in the Pacific in search of missing World War II boats and planes. Finding such artifacts is one thing. Finding information about those who died on board is far more important to him.

"That's why I have trouble with the 'archaeologist' thing," he said. "To label me an 'archaeologist' suggests that all I'm interested in is finding the plane. What I'm really interested in is tying these planes to the people who flew them."

Bert Smith didn't fly his plane.

His plane was piloted by Major Harry V. Scullin, commander of the VTMB-134 Torpedo Bomber Squadron. Corporal Matt L. Muller was the turret gunner. Bert was tail gunner and radio operator. That's

1

what The *Manchester Evening Leader* told its readers on Nov. 18, 1944, shortly after his parents learned he was missing in action.

"The local airman was a letterman in three sports, baseball, basketball and football at St. Joseph High School, where he was graduated in 1938," the paper reported.

"He entered the Marine Corps in February, 1943 and had never been home since that date, the family disclosed."

The brief newspaper account had one further disclosure: "Sergeant Smith is a brother of Ensign Edouard R. Smith, USN, who is stationed at the Naval Air Station in Jacksonville, Florida."

These days, Edouard R. Smith is better known to his friends and family in Manchester by his middle name, Rene. He's 76 now. He's the only surviving member of Bert Smith's immediate family and when he learned that his brother's plane had been discovered after all these years, the memories came flooding back.

He knows there are more to come.

"I'm already hearing things I've never heard before," Rene said. "I've always known very little of what happened to Bert. I made inquiry when I was down in Florida, but I had never even heard of Peleliu. It was meaningless to me. It was only a dot on a map and when I came home after the war, I think—with my parents—it was a case of them trying to forget. My mother took it very hard."

It's been hard on John Lally, too.

For 56 years, he's agonized over the fate of his friend. Even though he and Bert Smith grew up within a couple miles of one another in Manchester—Bert on Chester Street at the foot of Hanover Hill and John on Calef Road—it was only later, while in the service of their country, that they first met.

"We were on a train," said John, a 1941 Central High School graduate who was an aviation machinist's mate with VMF-121, a Marine fighter squadron.

"He had been training in Florida and our units were going across the country. I was headed to a base out there in the Mojave Desert in California. I don't know how we got to talking but we did. He said he was from Manchester. I said, 'Me too.'"

John Lally didn't know it, but Bert Smith told his parents all about that trip. He told them about the minutiae of the train ride; the banter, the meals, the towns they passed through. He told them about John Lally, too. It was all in a 28-page letter.

Bert's mother kept it. Rene Smith has it now.

"Supper in Mobile, Alabama," Bert wrote. "The food is good and all day was spent reading, sleeping and talking with the fellows. I met a fellow in the same car as me from Manchester. His name is Lally, a nice kid and we talked about home. The fellows are playing cards now but I've only three cents to my name so. . ."

The train ride wasn't the last Bert Smith and John Lally would see of each other.

They hooked up on a weekend pass in Santa Barbara. John smiles when he talks about it.

"We had a good time," he said. Of course, with his wife at his side, he's mum about the particulars—his grin has *Semper fi* written all over it—but soon after that liberty, they were both bound for the Pacific Theater.

"The bombers and the fighter planes traveled together," he explained, "and we both wound up in the New Hebrides Islands. I ran into Bert in the main village, Espiritu Santo. There were a few French-speaking settlers there and they made these hospitality houses for Marines and we had whatever beer we could scrounge up.

"That's where I found out Bert spoke French," he added. "He went to St. George's when he was a boy. He told me they spoke French at home, too."

Bert didn't get much chance to use his French in the New Hebrides.

In August of 1944, the Marine aviation units were off on a 2,000 mile voyage north through the Coral Sea en route to the Caroline Islands.

"We headed up to Guam for an over-nighter in the bay," John said, "then we formed the convoy that was going to hit Peleliu in the Western Carolines. I'm not sure when we arrived, but the first invasion was Sept. 15, and the planes didn't get to the island until after it was secured."

"Secured" is a word of nebulous meaning in the military.

Japanese troops were still dug in throughout the island. Even without their menacing presence, Peleliu—with its razor-sharp coral, impenetrable jungle and stifling heat—was hardly a welcoming environment. This from war correspondent Robert "Pepper" Martin of Time magazine:

"Peleliu is a horrible place," he wrote, "incomparably worse than

Guam in its bloodiness, terror, climate and the incomprehensible tenacity of the Japs. For sheer brutality and fatigue, I think it surpasses anything yet seen in the Pacific."

The numbers bear him out.

In two months, the Japanese had more than 10,000 casualties, all but a handful killed on an island roughly the size of East Manchester. More than 1,600 Marines were killed, another 7,000 wounded.

For 56 years, however, Bert Smith was neither. In time, he was listed as killed in action—the official declaration comes a year and a day after a disappearance—but to his family, he was missing.

Presumed dead, but missing.

Ever since Nov. 10, 1944.

"It was nighttime, and we had a scramble," John Lally said. "The whistles were going and everybody scrambled to get down to the flight line and into their planes and that night, there seemed to be a lot of action in the air.

"I remember there was some confusion on the runway. It was only one strip, but the fighters took off and then the bombers took off. There was only this one hill on the island. It was right at the end of the runway. That's where there were something like 15,000 Japanese hidden in the caves.

"That was their objective," he said. "The Marines called it Bloody Nose Ridge. That's where the Japanese had their anti-aircraft guns in these caves. They'd just roll them out and shoot and roll them back. They say it was the shortest bombing run in the war. The pilots didn't even put their flaps up when they took off. It was something like 1,400 yards to get up in the air, drop their load of napalm or five-hundred pounders, then turn back around."

Bert Smith's plane never made that turn.

"Down on the flight, line, we were watching for the planes as they came back," John said. "They were straggling back in. Finally, when it started getting light, I went back up to my tent. I was sitting around, waiting and hoping for news. Then a fellow from Bert's squadron came up and told me his plane didn't come in.

"It's hard to discern what your feelings are at that point," he said. "Of course you're angry. Then as the days pass, there's this sense of wondering. Are they down in the jungle? Are they coming back? Not knowing anything. That's the worst."

For 56 years, the family of Bert Smith experienced the worst.

(Originally published Sept. 10, 2000)

The Searchers

IT WAS 1993 WHEN DR. PATRICK SCANNON's voluntary research team discovered the hulk of a Japanese ship in the waters of the Pacific. The ship had been torpedoed in 1944 by a young Navy bomber pilot.

The pilot? Ensign George H. W. Bush.

With underwater cameras, the researchers panned over ammunition stores and gun mounts still visible on the deck of the sunken ship. The images proved that the ship was, in fact, a warship, enabling Scannon and his colleagues to dispel rumors that the future President of the United States had once attacked an unarmed trawler.

When that filmed footage was broadcast on ABC's "Nightline," Scannon was thrust into the national spotlight, but it was a native of Hanover, N.H.—Lewis "Chip" Lambert Jr.—who first thrust him under water.

Lambert, 56, is a microbiologist by vocation. Like Scannon, he works for Xoma, a pharmaceutical technology firm in Berkeley, California. His avocation—one of them, anyway—is scuba diving. Through that avocation, the two men have seized the public imagination with their unique form of military archaeology.

"When you're born and raised in the mountains of New Hampshire, it's a given that one of your interests is going to be skiing," he said, "but I also own a dive shop in San Jose. When I went to work at Xoma, I started offering scuba class to the other folks and Pat came along."

He also came along when Lambert started taking tour groups to the Palau Islands on scuba diving trips and when other friends entered the mix—friends like Dan Bailey, who was working on a book of World War II ship wrecks—their mutual interests began to mesh.

"In the beginning, I think the reason we went forward with this

Hanover native Lewis "Chip" Lambert was with the volunteer team that visited Peleliu Island and uncovered physical evidence of a missing torpedo bomber, evidence that may solve a mystery 50 years in the making. (Photo by Pamela Lewis)

stuff was the adventure and the enjoyment of solving these military mysteries," said Lambert, whose wife Pam is a charter member of the team. "In retrospect, the really interesting part is meeting and talking to some of these men who were involved in World War II.

"It's a shame it's taken so long to gain this appreciation for what they went though. Sometimes I feel like a little kid, sitting at their knee listening to their stories. It's a way for us to participate, vicariously, and in a case like this one, maybe bring them some amount of fulfillment."

Fulfillment is all Lambert and Scannon get. There are no tangible rewards for their work. There are no government subsidies, either. They pay their own way, but they do so willingly.

"It costs no more than if you were going to go on a dive vacation somewhere and look at pretty fish," said Lambert, whose father—Dr. Lewis Lambert Sr.—was an anesthesiologist at Mary Hitchcock Memorial Hospital in Hanover.

"We just put all our money in a pot and we go," he said. "It's a hell of a lot more interesting and exciting and educational than anything you could do as a tourist. Yes, it is expensive, but at the same time, the rewards are so much greater than you could possibly imagine."

Their next excursion? It leaves next month.

(9/10/00)

The wreckage of Bert Smith's Avenger torpedo bomber was discovered on Peleliu Island by Dr. Patrick Scannon and his volunteer crew of military archaeologists. (Photo by Lewis Lambert).

The Discovery

THE TERSE WESTERN UNION TELEGRAM—the telegram that every parent learned to dread—reached the East Manchester home of William and Mary Smith on Nov. 15,1944.

"DEEPLY REGRET TO INFORM YOU THAT YOUR SON SERGEANT BERTRAND L SMITH USMC IS MISSING IN ACTION IN THE PERFORMANCE OF DUTY TO HIS COUNTRY. I REALIZE YOUR GREAT ANXIETY BUT DETAILS NOT NOW AVAILABLE. . .

For 56 years, the details were not available.

Now they are.

Some of them, anyway.

The details began to emerge last June. That's when Dr. Patrick Scannon headed his small team into a dense mangrove swamp on Peleliu Island. He was fighting two elements: time and tide, which wait for no man. Not even a man who is spending his own time and money to find long-lost ships and planes from World War II.

"Filling in a page of history," he calls it.

For seven years, it's been his passion.

That's what keeps bringing him back to Peleliu Island, a 3-by-6-mile patch of coral in the Palau Island chain, one of many that freckle the Western Pacific expanse known as Micronesia.

"When we go to Peleliu," he said, "there's a person there, Tangi Hesus. He's a young man, but he's sort of the local World War II historian. He knew we were looking for planes this time, and he told us two fishermen who were hunting for crabs had come upon a crash site on this godforsaken part of the island."

Godforsaken or not, it was a part of the island that Scannon had to see, along with members of his team, including friend and colleague Chip Lambert, a Hanover native, and Lambert's wife, Pam.

"The three of us got in this flat-bottomed boat with some Palaun guides and the fishermen, and we headed into the mangroves," he said. "We had one free board above the water-line—maybe an inch—but we were racing against the low tide. We had to go in at high tide and get out before the tide went out, or we'd be stuck.

"Even with that, we had to jump out of the boat when we got close. We were chest deep in the muck, and we just started walking where they were pointing. From 20 feet, you would have missed it. The jungle there is extremely dense. We have this mantra: 'If they were easy to find, somebody else would have found it,' but how they found it, I'll never know."

What they found was the wreckage of a TMB-1C Avenger, a Marine torpedo bomber. The last time John Lally saw that same plane, it was clearing the end of the airstrip and heading toward the low rise of Umurbrogol Mountain.

His friend, Bert Smith, was manning the tail gun.

It was Nov. 10, 1944, and Japanese activity around the jumbled coral peak of the island—the Marines dubbed it Bloody Nose Ridge—had triggered the nighttime scramble. It took all of 15 seconds for the Marine torpedo bomber to reach the ridge, but what happened in those 15 seconds—and in the moments thereafter—would haunt John Lally for 56 years.

The plane disappeared without a trace.

"Not knowing anything," John said, "that's the worst."

A year later, much had changed. The war had ended, for one thing, but Bert Smith was still missing. So was his plane, so when John Lally returned to Manchester—hard as it was—he went to see Bert Smith's parents.

"It was right when I got out of the service in November of 1945," he said. "I spoke to his mother. She seemed very old. You could see she was still distraught over the whole thing. She had his picture in every doorway."

The same scene greeted Rene Smith when he returned from the war a month later. His older brother was gone. His parents were still trying to cope with the loss.

"When I came home, I guess it was a case of forgetting," said Rene, who—having spent the war as a Naval aviator flying planes off the deck of carriers such as the Intrepid and the Guadalcanal—had never heard of John Lally.

"When you're in the service and your brother is, too . . . well, I guess you're more matter-of-fact about it, maybe because you're facing danger yourself. Maybe it's one of the things you come to accept, more than if you're sitting at home waiting for news."

The waiting never ended for Bert Smith's parents.

They died without ever knowing what fate had befallen their first-born son. John Lally wanted desperately to avoid that same fate, so when he attended a Marine Corps reunion in Branson, Mo., last September, he approached the keynote speaker, a man billed as "the Indiana Jones of military archaeology."

It was Dr. Patrick Scannon.

"When John told me he had this friend who may have been shot down in a plane on Peleliu, it took me awhile to piece it together," he said, "but I knew we had shots of this Avenger, so he gave me a lead. That's better than nothing at all. I had a name, Bert Smith, which I took to the Navy Research Center."

By itself, the name would prove nothing. However, Dr. Scannon had something more. It was a number: 45946.

"The Bureau of Navy Aviation assigned a number to each plane by type, and even though the plane we found on Peleliu was busted up, there was a bureau number on the vertical stabilizer of the tail. With that, I was able to go back to the Navy Historical Research Center. Once I knew who was on the plane—Bert Smith—I contacted the appropriate authorities to get the appropriate personnel files."

Information on Bert Smith was in an 18-page Individual Deceased Personnel File. It documented efforts to find his body and those of his two crewmates, pilot Harry V. Scullin and turret gunner Matt L. Muller. There is little in the way of revelation, except the notation that Muller's body was found on Nov. 18,1944.

It was on a reef, far from the wreckage Scannon found in the jungle. It is here where Scannon has to engage in some conjecture, some speculation and some educated guessing, all of which—as a man of science—he prefers to avoid.

"The one thing we know for sure is that this is the plane they were flying," he said. "The bureau number is our anchor for that. How Muller's body could have shown up miles away? The simplest explanation is that he was able to bail out. When we found the wreck, there was no sign of the canopy. It's possible they all bailed out."

Possible, but unlikely.

As the tail gunner, Bert Smith was wedged in a small compartment in the rear of the plane. John Lally saw men squeeze their way inside those compartments. Even though Bert was a compact 5 feet 6—he weighed 165 pounds—it would have been difficult to extricate himself quickly.

Scannon estimates the duration of their flight at less than two minutes—the wreckage was about two miles from the airfield—and moderate shrapnel damage to the aft section of the aircraft raises further doubt about the likelihood of Bert's escape.

"Where we are right now, when we were on the plane, there was no evidence of human remains," Scannon said. "The plane had two levels, one for the pilot and turret and one below for the tail gunner, and we couldn't get to the lower level. Because we couldn't get there—we had a window of about two hours before we lost the tide—we can't rule out the possibility that his remains are still there."

Thus, what remains for Bert Smith's brother, Rene—a thoughtful, soft-spoken man—is to put the recent discovery into a personal context.

"I've been going through Bert's things again," he said, "the pictures and the telegrams and the letters. There was this one letter he wrote to my parents, it was 28 pages long, and I don't recall ever having seen that letter before. It gave me such an insight, the sensitivity he showed toward my parents.

"You have to bear in mind that I was five years younger than my brother, and at that age, five years is a big gap," he added. "I was always his kid brother, so I never got to know him from a man-to-man standpoint, simply because I wasn't a man yet. So for me, it's been nice to talk with someone who knew him so well.

"What's surprised me most through this whole thing is that John Lally knew so much about me, that he even knew to look for me with this news. You don't get a lot of praise from your older brother when you're growing up, but now I realize he had a different regard for me.

"I don't know. Maybe it's because I went in the service first, but I guess I reached a different status in his mind. To him, maybe I wasn't a kid anymore, but we never had the occasion for Bert to tell me that. John Lally was able to tell me that."

As chance would have it, John Lally's Marine squadron is going to hold a reunion in Maine this week. The men of VMF-121 have social events planned for Old Orchard Beach tomorrow and Wednesday, and on Thursday, they'll gather at the Middle School in Saco at 11 a.m. to hear from their keynote speakers, Dr. Patrick Scannon and Chip Lambert.

Rene Smith was invited.

He politely declined.

In the last few weeks, he's come to know the love and regard his brother had for him—perhaps it's something he needed to know for 56 years—and he also knows he has another brother of sorts in John Lally.

"That's what's been meaningful for me," Rene said. "It's not the fact that they recovered his plane. The plane couldn't tell me anything about Bert. John could."

It's been an emotional odyssey for both men.

"To meet Rene ... I was just overwhelmed," John said. "He's a very gracious fellow, and he's so very grateful I was able to find him with this information. He's always lived with this, wondering about his brother.

"Now he knows. Now I know."

(9/11/00)

The Keene American Legion Band includes, from left, trumpeter Andy Davis, Sousaphonist Barbara George and brass players Bob Whitney, Mickey Arceci and Don Strange. (Union Leader Photo by John Clayton)

And The Band Played On

FOR YEARS NOW, my friend Andy Davis has been after me to do a story about the Keene American Legion Band but apparently, I've been busy marching to the beat of my own drummer.

It's not that I think Andy's trying to toot his own horn—he plays the trumpet, by the way—but mostly, it's because I haven't been able to catch the band in action. I finally managed to catch up with the band on Sunday at Manchester's Jutras Post.

And I still haven't caught my breath.

You want to talk about a band on the run?

Let's talk about this band from the Gordon-Bissell Post 4 in Keene. Since this snappy marching ensemble made its first appearance at the 1946 Memorial Day parade in Keene, it has appeared in thousands of parades. This year is no exception. Before it shuts down for the season on Veterans Day, the band will have played 35 dates this year and there are 40 more bookings already set for the year 2000.

Clearly, there's no such thing as "parade rest" for this group.

"We're one of the last marching Legion bands in New Hampshire," said Gene Gober, a tuba-toting 81-year-old who has been with the band since day one. "And you know, for something to last more than 50 years, you have to have a pretty good bond."

And this band has bonded from the get-go.

Consider this 1946 review—and note the astonishing economy of language—that was published in the Keene Evening Sentinel: "They play in good tune. They are a credit to the Legion. They will go places."

Have they ever.

In the 54 years of the band's existence, parade venues have ranged from Fifth Avenue in New York to Bourbon Street in New Orleans to

Kalakaua Avenue on Waikiki Beach in Honolulu. Its members have played at the 1965 New York World's Fair and at the dedication of the Vietnam Veterans Memorial in Washington, D.C.

They even played at the first Sweepstakes Race at Rockingham Park in 1964, although famed sportscaster Red Barber found it ironic that gamblers were swarming to the betting windows even as the band played "Onward, Christian Soldiers."

"That wasn't supposed to happen," laughed Bob Whitney, 75, another of the band's charter members, "but the drum major was over at the window himself. When he heard us fire that up, well, I thought he was going to explode."

That minor gaffe aside, the band has always won favor for its music. It is also renowned for its pluck. Members like to cite the tercentenary parade in Deerfield, Mass., back in 1973 when more than 200 people—and one elephant—were felled by the 100-degree temperatures.

Not so our local heroes. Quoth the Springfield Union: "A mostly World War II American Legion Post Band from Keene, N.H. was the only unit to look sharp when it passed the finish line about 5:30."

Troupers that they are, band members know that the show must go on. But there's show business, and then there's show business. That's something they learned the hard way when, back in 1971, they were asked to take part in the filming of a movie called "A Separate Peace."

Since the movie was to be set in the 1940s, the fashionably long hair of the '70s was a problem for the producers, who asked that band members be shorn of their long locks. Most agreed—many reluctantly—and then they spent the afternoon playing and marching before the cameras on the campus at Phillips Exeter Academy.

Stardom? Hardly. In the parlance of Hollywood, their performance wound up on the cutting room floor. Bad music? Nope. Bad planning. The film's producers failed to get signed release forms from the band members.

"We told everyone to go see the movie so they could see what stars we were," smiled Gene, "and they're still looking for us. I still have a copy of the check they gave me for being an extra, though. It was for twenty-five bucks."

For all of those star-spangled bookings, though, the true heart and soul of the Keene American Legion Band is on display at the countless small-town celebrations that make life in New Hampshire so . . . well, so New Hampshire-like.

One day, it could be the opening of a Legion post in Hillborough, then it's a Fourth Of July parade in Jaffrey or it's a "Concert on the Green" in Walpole. The role is that of the small-town band, and it's a role that fewer and fewer are willing to play. That means the band is always seeking new members.

"The shame is that there are so few ways for the different generations to communicate," said Bob. "As I get older, I realize more and more how our music is a medium that can bring all ages together.

"My wife says if I'm going to work this hard—I'm retired—I should go back and make some money, but I think it's important to preserve this kind of tradition."

Another tradition for this band is its status as a professional melting pot.

"Well, I was a school teacher," Gene said, "and Peter Dumont is a priest and David Proper is an historian and Gene Gaffey was a judge and we have a watchmaker and a psychologist and one of the girls just became a lawyer. It seems like we have a little bit of everything, but once we get out on the street, we're not individuals. We're one unit."

People can see that unit in action when the band takes part in the Keene Firefighters' Parade. Perhaps as people watch and listen, they may come to understand that the harmony of this unit extends far beyond the music.

That closeness, that camaraderie was on display over Labor Day weekend, when the band traveled to the American Legion National Convention in Anaheim, Calif. On the morning of the big parade, beloved band manager Bill Olmstead—who had been with the band since 1948—suffered a heart attack and died in his hotel room.

Stunned band members struggled with their shock and grief. Many asked the question that had to be asked.

"You could see that a lot of people were having a hard time dealing with it," said my friend Andy, who joined the band at the age of 12—that was 27 years ago—and is still referred to as "one of the new guys."

"People started to ask whether we should take part in the parade that afternoon, and someone said 'Of course we're going to go. That's what he'd want us to do.'"

It was a tribute to Bill Olmstead.

And the band played on.

(9/30/99)

Friends and classmates wanted to make certain that Major Gerald R. Helmich was remembered in the West Manchester neighborhood where he grew up. (Photo Courtesy of Donn Inglis)

War... and Remembrance

IT'S BEEN 30 YEARS—nearly half a lifetime—since Major Gerald R. Helmich's plane crashed into the jungles of Laos. Thirty long years. Long enough, perhaps, for his memory to fade from the thoughts of neighbors and casual acquaintances.

Not for Donn Inglis.

Donn still remembers his high school classmate—West High, 1950—and today, on Memorial Day, others will remember Jerry Helmich too.

They're dedicating a plaque in Jerry's memory today at 1 p.m. It will stand at the corner of Second Street and West Hancock in the West Manchester neighborhood where Jerry grew up.

"It all started when we began working on our 50th reunion," Donn said. "Since Jerry was the only member of our class to die in military service, I thought it might be nice to have a small display about him at the reunion."

Before long, Donn's project turned into a mission.

Jerry Helmich's final mission was about life and death.

Then again, they all were.

He was an Air Force pilot with the 6th Special Operations Squadron based at Pleiku, a small airbase in the Central Highlands of Vietnam. His unit, the 633rd Special Operations Wing, was often deployed to help save downed pilots. In military shorthand, it's called SAR—search and rescue.

That was his mission on Nov. 12, 1969.

"We heard that a plane had gone down but the pilots had made radio contact, so they were organizing a rescue mission for them," said Dr. Amos Townsend of Lee, who was commander of the medical facility at Pleiku Air Base. "I remember it was on a Sunday morning, so I just headed down to the field and Jerry came by and said he was one of the ones going out."

It wasn't the first time.

Since being posted to Vietnam in June, he had been on dozens of similar missions in his single-engine Spad, an A-1H Skyraider. Two months earlier, he had won the Distinguished Flying Cross. A month later he picked up an Air Medal and a second DFC. The job wasn't about medals though. It was about men.

The distress call had come from the crew of an F-4 Phantom dubbed "Owl 07." The fighter had gone down just before dawn, 11 miles south of the Mu Gia Pass, a major branch of the Ho Chi Minh Trail just across the Vietnamese border in Southern Laos.

It was territory controlled by the enemy.

"The F-4 crew was on the ground near a river, hidden as well as they could manage, from the North Vietnamese troops in the area," said Capt. Charlie Holder, a pilot based in nearby Thailand who joined Jerry and six other A-1 pilots in the complex search and rescue mission.

"The reason we knew there were enemy troops in the area was that at least two, maybe three more aircraft had been hit since the initial Owl 07 loss," he added. "Those crews had managed to nurse their planes over a 'safe ejection area' a few miles away. In short though, this was a real hot area."

Jerry knew what the pilots were going through on the ground.

Like all of the pilots in the area, he too had gone through the fabled "Snake School" at Clark Field in the Philippines. The pilots jokingly referred to it as "tropical adaptation." The Air Force called it what it was: "jungle survival training."

By mid-morning, eight A-1's converged on the area where the downed pilots had taken refuge, four more than the normal complement. Their role was to support the "Jolly Green Giants"—the H-3 helicopters that would touch down to retrieve the downed flyers—by neutralizing enemy guns with fire from above and by laying down heavy phosphorous smoke screens to shield the vulnerable choppers from ground fire.

It was that same ground fire that brought down Jerry's plane.

Captain Holder was 500 feet off his tail when it happened.

"We practiced these 'Daisy Wheels' as a flight of four," he said. "Now, we were trying to set up an eight-ship 'Daisy Wheel' over the survivors, in a valley, under 'contested' conditions.

"Confusion reigned," he said, and when another A-1 pulled up in front of him, Captain Holder surrendered his spot and fell back in the formation. The plane that took his place began taking ground fire at 500 feet.

"Whatever it was, it truly nailed the aircraft in front of me," he said, "the aircraft that, seconds earlier, had taken my place in the pattern. There was no fire or explosion, but the aircraft rolled to the right to an inverted position and crashed."

It was only later that Captain Holder learned that the pilot who crashed—a classmate from "Snake School"—was Jerry Helmich.

The pilots they set out to save were eventually rescued, but after Jerry's plane went down—according to military documents—"No SAR attempt was made."

It would be nearly nine years before the Air Force finally declared that Jerry Helmich had been killed in action. He had been promoted twice in those nine years, first to lieutenant colonel in 1973 and then to full colonel in 1978.

A memorial service, attended by his wife and three children, was held on Dec. 3, 1978, at Dobbins Air Force Base in Georgia. He was posthumously awarded the Purple Heart and the Silver Star. A marker bearing his name was placed in the cemetery there.

His body has never been found.

Attempts were made, however. In October of 1994, a 10-man team from Laos and the United States traveled to Khammouan Province. Using the coordinates of Jerry's last known position, they went to Ban Senphan and interviewed the village elders.

Documents released by the Defense Department and the Joint Task Force-Full Accounting offered conflicting accounts on his case, listed as #1521. In one interview, a witness told investigators that a pilot's body had once been buried by a villager named "Lung Kut," but others denied ever knowing such a man. In the end, the analyst offered this terse conclusion:

"Due to the vast number of losses in this area, it is difficult to correlate any one case. With no firsthand witnesses, no specific crash sites . . . it is not possible to correlate this to case #1521."

The details of Jerry's last mission were pieced together by Donn Inglis. First he visited Jerry's stepmother with another West High classmate, Kay Bayko. Then he wrote to directors of the Vietnam Veterans Memorial in Washington. Later on, Dr. Townsend put him in contact with the historian from the Pleiku Air Base Association, who provided the names and addresses of Jerry's fellow pilots.

Over time, via letters and e-mail, his story took shape.

"In the beginning, I was just trying to get a story in the paper for the 30th anniversary of his death," Donn said. "I thought we might be able to put something up at the high school to let the kids know about this man who was educated at West High and at UNH who lost his life serving his country."

In the end, he got a lot more.

When Bob St. Onge from the Veterans of Foreign Wars Post 8214 got wind of the quest, he offered assistance. So did Mike Lopez from the Manchester Veterans Council. The New Hampshire chapter of the Northeast POW/MIA Network got involved, and so did the City of Manchester, which pledged to maintain the permanent marker that will help people remember Jerry Helmich.

From the outset, that's what it was all about. Donn Inglis wanted people to remember his friend. Today, of all days, it's important for us all to remember.

(5/31/99)

An Army of His Own

 WHAT DOES FRANK RICHARDS have in common with generals like George Washington and Robert E. Lee and Douglas MacArthur and Dwight D. Eisenhower and William Westmoreland and Norman Schwarzkopf?

He had his own army.

The difference?

Frank got his when he was 10 years old.

It was the Abbot Place Army, a tight-knit squadron of imaginative schoolboys who kept the citizens of Exeter safe from the Hun in the days during and after The War to End All Wars. Their theater of operation? The grounds of Phillips Exeter Academy, where, in 1920, their precocious maneuvers caught the eye of an aide to Gen. John J. "Black Jack" Pershing.

The aide's name?

History books refer to him as Gen. George C. Marshall.

If the name doesn't ring a bell, well, he was only the winner of the Nobel Peace Prize and the man most responsible for the resurrection of Europe after World War II, but that was only after he served in the far more important capacity as tactical adviser to the Abbot Place Army.

"Gen. Pershing was just back from the war," Frank explained. "He had come to Exeter to put his son in the academy. We called it the school for 'poor little rich boys.' While they were there, Col. Marshall heard we had an army and he thought it would be a very good idea if we got together for a parade review before Gen. Pershing, so we did. And we marched right past the both of them."

Today, on the eve of his 89th birthday, Frank Richards still embraces the moment as if happened yesterday.

"We were just a bunch of friends," he smiled, "and back then, we

The Veterans Home in Tilton is where Frank Richards maintains the small shrine that chronicles The Abbot Place Army. (Union Leader Photo by John Clayton)

kids played war because that's all we heard about. Dr. Lewis Perry was the headmaster at Phillips Exeter. His son, Lewis, and I were great friends, so I was the general of our army and Lewis was the second in command."

As he spoke, Frank fingered a folder full of clippings and mementos that cover the desk in his room at the Veterans Home in Tilton, where surely he is the only boyhood general in residence. Included in the pile on his desk are the confidential field orders he later received from then-Col. Marshall.

The objective?

Mark Twain should be telling this story.

They were out to defeat the army of Alton Jacobsen.

"Alton's father was a dentist who had just moved to town," wrote Lewis Perry Jr. in a reminiscence he penned for Yankee magazine in 1981. "And Alton, we felt, should have adopted a more mouselike facade until we got to know him better.

"This was not Alton's way," he added, "and just about the time it began to occur to some of us that he might be planning some sort of military attack, unbelievably—horror of horrors—he pushed me (the colonel in Frank's army!) out of the line one morning coming in from recess."

Certainly, wars have been fought over lesser transgressions.

It required an immediate response, so—without the benefit of Col. Marshall's counsel—the Abbot Place Army mobilized. With the spartan prose and stilted spelling of a 10-year-old, Frank Richards had long ago set forth his army's marching orders:

- Know taking or lafing.
- Know joks or faling.
- Keep in line.
- Mind good.
- Always have your ams.
- Mind your leders.
- Always when you spek to the head one, slute.

Rigorous guidelines indeed. Yet, when the battle was finally joined, it would be an understatement to say that our heroes in the Abbot Place Army were routed. In truth, the outcome was akin to Little Big Horn. Think Dunkirk, only worse.

All because the army of Alton Jacobsen had a secret weapon.

"When we arrived at the scene of the battle we found not just craven little Alton," wrote Lewis Perry, "but also Big Walt Gillespie, the older brother of one of our stalwarts, who proceeded to throw us into confusion, panic and retreat.

"Defeat had encompassed us," he added, "total and ignominious. And had it not been for Col. Marshall, that would have been the end of the war."

Not many 10-year-olds have a direct pipeline to military intelligence—then or now—but Col. Marshall was not about to abandon an army that had so impressed Black Jack Pershing. On his next visit to Exeter, Marshall met with the troops.

"You boys need a new weapon," he said.

"That was his precise phrase," Col. Perry recalled. "He followed us up into the attic that we used as a clubhouse and army headquarters, and there, after poking around a bit, he found a large collection of bamboo poles leaning in a dark corner.

"What you need," he said, "are spears and lances, and here they are!"

"He scarcely needed to brief us on their use," Perry noted, "It was obvious. And sure enough, in the ensuing confrontation, we scarcely needed our swords and shields. Big Walt was held at bay on three sides and Alton Jacobsen could be poked from a safe distance, to say nothing of the other little kids in the demoralized array that soon sought safety in flight."

They say the Battle of Waterloo was won on the playing fields of Eton, and, so it is that Frank Richards—at the tender age of 10—came to understand the role of the warrior class on the playgrounds of Exeter.

Of course, that was all unofficial.

His "official" military service began in 1943 when—as a 33-year-old father of two sons—he was the first married man in New Hampshire to be drafted into the Army. Some would have balked. He never blinked.

"Our ancestry goes back to the French and Indian War," he said. "There's been a Richards in every war since 1675. That's 100 years before the Revolution. We even had an ancestor, Joseph Richards, who was killed in the Rochester Indian Massacre in 1746, but in 1943, they needed men who knew a trade so I, along with my three brothers, all of us served in the Pacific theater.

"I won no citations or Purple Hearts, nor was I a hand-to-hand combat hero," said Frank, who was a dock construction foreman in the Philippines, "but I sweated out bombing and strafing and the call to battle stations under Japanese torpedo attacks, and with my brothers, I took part in the greatest war that man has ever fought."

He had his share of adventures before the war, too. He sowed his wild oats during the Depression and traveled the country by hopping freight trains. He worked on oil rigs in Texas and in rock mines in Colorado and in orange groves in Florida. Then he came home and married Miss Ella Higgins.

After the war, Frank did what so many other veterans did. He raised his family. He ran his construction business. He joined the Masons. He helped rebuild a church steeple in Stratham. He drove a school bus for handicapped kids in Newington. He built a firehouse in Greenland. He served in the Legislature. He was even named Citizen of the Year.

In short, his has been a rich and full life, so rich, in fact, that—to his mind—his boyhood interactions with Black Jack Pershing and George C. Marshall are little more than interesting footnotes.

"I loved my wife," he said. "She was a beautiful woman. We had three children, they all went to the University of New Hampshire— John, Thomas and Emily—and I'm terribly proud of them and my six grandchildren. I had good friends, too, and I served my country."

As he spoke, he eyed the photos on the wall of his room at the Veterans Home. It's a small room, but it's comfortable. It's probably the size of the clubhouse where his boyhood army mustered with George C. Marshall.

"Some people might think I'm lonely here," he smiled, "but I'm a happy man. They take good care of me here, especially the nurses. I feel secure here, but word is I'm looking for a widow with a small farm."

He winked.

"You see, now that I'm in the evening of my years, I don't drink, I don't smoke and I don't gamble, but I do still have a soft- spot for women."

And that's not a bad thing.

Generally speaking.

(10/21/99)

It took 50 years, but the creation of a monument in his hometown made certain that Rene Gagnon's role in history—a role played out at Iwo Jima—would forever be a point of pride. (Associated Press Photo by Joe Rosenthal/Inset Photo Courtesy of Mrs. Rene Gagnon)

Rene Gagnon

IT WAS BACK IN OCTOBER. They asked me to speak at a breakfast for the DARE program, so I wrote a speech about how kids need heroes and role models. It seemed appropriate.

I figured I could talk about some people I admire, local folks who overcame some hurdles to make their mark in the world. A lot of the names are probably familiar to you, like Richard McDonald and Grace Metalious, and to me, they're what hometown heroes are all about.

The speech went over well enough, I guess. People laughed when they were supposed to laugh and they applauded when it was time. Looking back on it, I realized I only made one mistake.

I forgot Rene Gagnon.

We do that a lot around here.

His image is frozen in the memory of every American who was alive in 1945 and, for those of us who've come along since, he's part of an indelible national symbol, yet somehow, we often forget to claim him as one of our own.

That won't happen anymore.

At 2 P.M. today, the Memorial Day parade will step off on Elm Street, and by 3 P.M., it's expected to wind its way to Victory Park. That's where they're going to unveil a monument to Rene Gagnon. After 50 years, he's finally getting some recognition where it matters most—in his hometown.

It's a symbolic gesture, to be sure—Rene died in 1979—but he learned the value of symbols on Feb. 23, 1945. That was the day he joined with four other U.S. Marines and a U.S. Navy corpsman and helped plant a flag in a volcanic ash heap called Mount Suribachi on the island of Iwo Jima.

Like all combat soldiers, these six were striving toward a common goal, but not with weapons of war. They were armed instead with the most powerful symbol of all—a flag—and the unforgettable image captured by AP photographer Joe Rosenthal made them symbols unto themselves.

The only problem? No one knew who they were.

Rosenthal had taken a series of photos that day and dispatched his film without ever seeing the finished product. When the photo began running on front pages all over America—it showed up in *The Manchester Leader* on Feb. 26—everyone wanted to know their names.

War has little patience, however, for the vagaries of public relations, and, as if to punctuate the savagery of the fighting on Iwo Jima, three of the six were dead within a week of the flag raising. Mindful of morale on the homefront, military officials tracked down the survivors—a Pima Indian from Arizona named Ira Hayes, U.S. Navy Pharmacist's Mate John Bradley from Appleton, Wisconsin, and Rene Gagnon—and immediately ordered them stateside.

Even in a more innocent media age, Rene made great copy. He was right out of Queen City central casting—a French-Canadian kid who had to leave Central High School after two years to work in the mills. He tried to join the U.S. Navy at 17 but was refused for high blood pressure. When he finally got into the U.S. Marine Corps, he kept a picture of his sweetheart—Pauline Harnois—in his helmet, and on the way home, he told reporters he couldn't wait to taste his mom's cooking again.

The reason for his homecoming wasn't entirely sentimental. Along with Hayes and Bradley, he was sent on a barnstorming tour of America. Thanks in part to the star power of the Iwo Jima veterans, the Seventh War Bond Drive raised $220 million for the war effort.

By August of 1945, the media crush began to subside. Shortly after V-J Day, Rene was back in the Pacific in combat fatigues, serving with U.S. occupational forces in China. After his discharge in 1946, he was back home with Pauline—America had dubbed her "the sweetheart of Iwo Jima"—and he was back in the spinning room at Chicopee Manufacturing. He couldn't have been farther away from the spotlight.

And he couldn't have been happier.

"To tell you the truth, he was uncomfortable about all that hero stuff," said Omer Gagnon, a childhood friend from St. George's School and The Corporation who saw plenty of action himself at Omaha Beach and Salerno. "The way we saw it, the only hero was a dead hero. They're the ones who gave their lives for their country."

Attention still came Rene's way—there was even a cameo role in the John Wayne film *Sands of Iwo Jima*—yet there were subtle twists of fate, strange mergers of chance and coincidence that seemingly conspired against him.

In the historic photo itself, Rene is largely obscured by the figure of John Bradley, and it wasn't the last time he would be denied his moment in the sun.

Even in the history books, his legacy is frequently garbled. In *Iwo Jima: Legacy of Valor*, for instance, author Bill D. Ross describes Rene as being from "New Hampshire's Green Mountains."

But most importantly, it was when his moment of glory was at hand in his hometown that the fates intervened most cruelly.

When the U.S. Marine Corps ordered him home in April of 1945, the Queen City was in a frenzy. The reception planned in his honor was described as "the biggest homecoming welcome in the history of Manchester." First there was to be a banquet at the Carpenter Hotel, then an evening parade down Elm Street followed by a massive gathering at Bronstein Park.

Dignitaries throughout New Hampshire were clamoring to share the stage with Rene Gagnon. Legionnaires and Cub Scouts alike were lobbying for spots in the parade and for a solid week, the newspaper whipped the city into a patriotic lather. Just when it seemed like his day would never come, it arrived at last. April 12, 1945.

And Franklin Delano Roosevelt died.

The crowds that had lined Elm Street waiting to cheer Rene Gagnon stood in stunned silence as police cars with bull horns broadcast the tragic news. The celebration was canceled. Before it began, Rene's party was over.

Only now, some 50 years later, is he getting his due.

Maybe he would have preferred it that way. After all, he once told a reporter "I'd rather face another invasion operation than go on the bond tour," but in his absence, people like Hubie McDonough Jr. and Don Duhamel and Mike Lopez have made certain that future generations will know of his special place in American history.

For the record, Rene Gagnon is buried in Arlington National Cemetery. His body lies in Section 51 Grave 543—just one more headstone in a sea of 181,000 identical white markers—but as of May 29, 1995, he will be remembered in Manchester forever thanks to the monument that stands, fittingly enough, in the shadow of the American flag.

(5/29/95)

Their success in shooting down deadly Iraqi missiles made sure that Bow's Michael Nieder (third from left) and his U.S. Army battery mates would gain national renown as "Scudbusters." (Associated Press Photo)

The Bow "Scudbuster"

 FOR A FEW HOURS LAST NIGHT, the yellow ribbons came down and the red carpet was rolled out as the town of Bow extended a hero's welcome to one of its own.

Sgt. Michael Nieder, whose Patriot missile unit shot down four Scud missiles over Saudi Arabia on Jan. 21, 1991, was greeted by more than 100 friends and well-wishers at a hastily assembled reception at the Grist Mill Restaurant.

The 20-year-old Army Commendation Medal winner was clearly stunned by the reception, and as he stepped from the family van, a cheer erupted from the crowd as Nieder was mauled by his high school buddies.

It didn't take long for tears to mix with the cheers, as Nieder's emotional response to the outpouring of support triggered the same response amongst those who had gathered to welcome him home.

Tears streamed down his cheeks as he willingly signed the guest register at the Grist Mill and again as he accepted a box of Girl Scout cookies from nine-year-old Caitlin Whalley of Bow, his pen-pal when he was in Saudi Arabia.

"I just want to thank you all for coming," Nieder said, after receiving a number of small gifts. "We all appreciate your support, and that was our biggest fear.

"We just didn't want to be hated for what we were doing. We don't make the decisions. We just fight the wars. We all volunteered and I think it was the right thing to do. There's still some hard work to be done there and if I have to, I'll go again."

With Nieder's remarks concluded, Gary Gordon of the Concord Chapter of the Vietnam Veterans of America stepped forward and handed Nieder a glass of beer.

"Welcome home," he said. "I hope you're old enough."

Nieder didn't bother to respond, and he dispatched the beer the same way his unit dispatched Scud missiles with such effectiveness while serving with Charlie Company, 3rd Battalion, 43rd Air Defense Artillery Regiment.

Although he was aware of the rallies held in support of U.S. troops in the Persian Gulf, Nieder said American servicemen were also aware of anti-war rallies, which concerned them.

"We knew there was a lot of support, but I never knew there'd be this much," he said, as he nodded toward the room.

The crowd was assembled on such short notice because of the organization known as SOS—Send Our Support.

"I got a call from Mike's mother at 9:30 (Sunday) night," said Bobbie Terrill of Bow, one of the founders of SOS. "Mike had just called from Fort Bliss in Texas and told her he'd be home Monday at 6:00, so we had to get moving.

"We have our own telephone tree, so we started making calls and I called the local Vietnam vets who have their own telephone tree, and this is what we came up with on less than 24 hours notice."

Although there was extra excitement because Nieder was the first of 13 Bow residents to return home from the Gulf, the members of SOS have vowed to welcome the others home in similar fashion and also to continue their work in support of the troops.

"Mike is the first of many to come home, but there are still kids who will be there for two to four more months, and they still need our support," said Terrill. "People are already forgetting about them, but there's a lot of dangerous work that still lies ahead."

Meanwhile, Sgt. Nieder, flanked by his parents, Coral and Roy Nieder, was presented with several gifts, including a Desert Storm cap, a plaque proclaiming him "New Hampshire's Number One Scudbuster," a massive cake repeating the Scudbuster theme and a letter of welcome from Gov. Judd Gregg.

"You have served our nation with courage and dignity, and like all of the New Hampshire men and women in our armed forces during the Persian Gulf War, you have made us very proud," the governor wrote.

Also looking on with pride were veterans of another conflict, the Vietnam veterans who have been such a source of support for the families of servicemen stationed in the Persian Gulf.

"We made a decision at the local and national level that what happened to us when we came home would never happen to anyone ever again," said Gordon. "We vowed to do whatever we could to make sure these men and women were welcomed when they came home, and obviously, it's working."

(3/12/91)

SERGT. GEORGE F. ROBIE,
Co. D.

The final resting place of Candia native George Frank Robie, a Medal of Honor recipient, is born anew thanks to a Civil War scholar in Galveston, Texas. (Union Leader File Photo by Dick Morin)

A Grave Oversight

THE PEOPLE OF NEW HAMPSHIRE take pride in remembering their veterans, and not just on Memorial Day. It's like that in Texas, too.

George Frank Robie would attest to that, if he could.

He can't, though. The Candia native died more than a century ago, but not before making his mark in the service of his country.

For many of those years since his death, he lay in relative anonymity, more than a thousand miles from home. His grave was marked by a dull, gray headstone, aged and weathered by a century of scorching Texas heat and the sea air that blows through Galveston off the Gulf of Mexico.

That didn't sit well with some folks in Texas—Daniel Lisarelli in particular—which is why Robie's old gravestone is gone. Today, his final resting place is marked by a gleaming, white marble marker with embossed gold lettering.

It's only fitting for a Medal of Honor recipient.

It was the installation of that new headstone that brought a solemn ceremony to the New City Cemetery in Galveston back in November, and Houston resident Kenneth Graham thought we ought to know about it.

"We Texans are justifiably proud of our military heritage, from the Alamo to Desert Storm," he said, "but we also know that valor is not a regional attribute, and we applaud bravery in any man."

Perseverance is another admirable attribute, and it is a trait that Lisarelli—a 37-year-old middle school computer teacher—shared with Robie.

Lisarelli is a Civil War scholar. He was descended from a Pennsylvania family with a proud tradition of service to the Union Army. He even serves with a group known as the Sons of Union Veterans of the

Civil War, and sometime last year, he got to wondering whether any Union Medal of Honor winners might have settled in the area he now calls home.

"I'd been doing research on Camp Groce, a small POW camp near Hempstead, Texas," he said. "There was a Medal of Honor recipient from the Union Army who was held prisoner there, so I got hold of the Medal of Honor book to look him up.

"Since I had it, I figured I'd look for any other local bits and I came across the name of George Frank Robie. It said he'd died in Galveston, but it didn't say where he was buried."

Lisarelli figured Robie's body had been shipped back to New Hampshire, but just in case, he decided to roam through the New City Cemetery.

"I didn't expect much," he said. "There was a bad hurricane here in 1900, and they brought in fill to raise the island 15 feet. If you didn't pay for someone's grave to be raised, it stayed where it was, and since he didn't have family here, I never thought I'd find anything."

But, after a day of roaming through the graveyard, he came upon something that was enough to invoke the name of the Lord.

"I said, 'My God,' and my jaw hit the ground," Lisarelli said. "It was just this flat, dull gray headstone. His grave was marked after all. Barely, but it was marked."

Finding Robie's gravesite was a triumph. Finding out about his personal history and his war record was far more problematic for Lisarelli. Details are few. Even his Medal of Honor citation—typical of the Civil War era—merely states: "Gallantry on the skirmish line."

At the outbreak of the Civil War, we know that Robie first enlisted with the Eighth Massachusetts Infantry for a three-month hitch, a term deemed sufficient to quell the uprising. When the war continued, his parents—Nathaniel and Ruth Robie—brought him to Manchester where, on Sept. 25, 1861, he signed on for three years with Company D of the 7th Regiment, New Hampshire Volunteer Infantry.

He was mustered in as a sergeant. After three months training, he was promoted to first sergeant. He was wounded in battle at Olustee, Fla., but recovered sufficiently to undertake a reconnaissance mission near the besieged Confederate capital of Richmond, Va., in September of 1864. It was there where his conspicuous bravery won him a promotion to lieutenant. It also won him a Medal of Honor nomination.

It took 19 years for Congress to act upon that nomination, 19 years that Lisarelli has also tried to piece together.

His research revealed that Robie arrived in Galveston in 1869, where the census listed him as a store clerk. Later, he worked as a bookkeeper with the railroad, but Lisarelli suspects those jobs were merely ways to pass the days. He thinks Robie had a drinking problem—his death certificate says he died of liver disease—tied to his wounds and his war experience.

"I think the poor fella was in such pain, he drank to alleviate it," Lisarelli said. "He did apply for a military pension. There was an affidavit in his pension file from a woman in Lowell, Mass. I think it might have been a woman he'd wanted to marry, but she described him as 'a used-up man' because he was so disabled."

In the end, Robie died—alone—on June 10, 1891.

However, instead of his death, it was his life that was remembered on Veterans Day last November when the Medal of Honor Historical Society placed a new headstone on Robie's grave. Buglers and bagpipers lent solemnity to the ceremony and two Vietnam-era Medal of Honor winners, Green Beret Ray Benevidez and Army medic Clarence Sassier, unveiled the new stone.

Looking on was Lisarelli.

"I was prepared to pay for the headstone myself," he said, "but the man from Ott Monument Works wouldn't let me. He said to me, 'How many times do you get to do this for a Medal of Honor winner?'"

Gestures like that—gestures that surround the rediscovery of Robie's grave—are sure to resonate with New Hampshire folks.

"I am frankly honored that they would even think of doing such a thing," said Phyllis Longver of Webster, who researches the records of New Hampshire's Civil War veterans. "He may have died forgotten in Texas with no one to mourn him, and now this. I think it's splendid."

George Frank Robie is now remembered in Galveston, and if Daniel Lisarelli has his way, he never will be forgotten.

"He's my hero," he said. "I drive past his grave every day on the way to work, and I am so proud. It's a heavy responsibility, but I'll do my best to keep it and maintain it for the rest of my life."

(5/25/98)

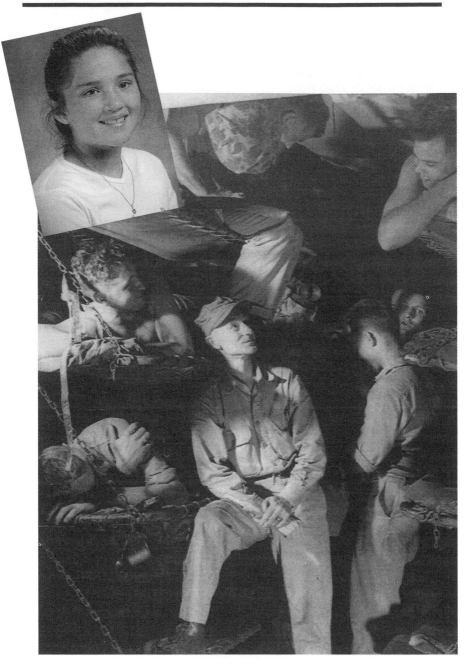

*The work of famed war correspondent Ernie Pyle captured the imagi-
nation of Erin Kane (inset) who sought out New Hampshire men
who were included in his World War II dispatches. (Associated Press
Photo/Inset Courtesy of Erin Kane)*

Ernie Pyle and Citizen Kane

NO MATTER WHAT YOUR TEACHER friends may tell you, kids don't read as much as they used to. That's why, when you find a 12-year-old who's been thumbing through a book of old newspaper columns by Ernie Pyle, the first thing you do is marvel at the thought. Then you give in to human nature and ask the obvious question.

Why?

That's what I asked Erin Kane.

"Because it looked interesting," she said.

That's when I knew I was in the company of a pretty interesting kid.

Erin's a sixth grader at Hillside Middle School in Manchester. She's been reading a book called "Ernie's War." It's a collection of columns and dispatches Ernie Pyle wrote during World War II.

Six days a week, in 310 newspapers for more than 12 million readers, Pyle set out to talk to average GIs and provide what he called "a worm's-eye-view" of the war. He did just that. In the process—in case you're too young to remember him—he also fashioned some of the most indelible prose of the last century.

Erin is too young to remember—she's too young to remember Desert Storm, for that matter—but she's not too young to appreciate good writing, and when she came across a passage where Ernie Pyle crossed paths with a soldier from Manchester, well, she wanted to know more.

She dropped me a line.

"One of the names mentioned was a Private John Coughlin of Manchester, New Hampshire," her e-mail said. "I was interested in finding out more about him and what happened to him in the war."

It's not like she didn't try to find out on her own.

"I have looked at Manchester West High School yearbooks dating back to 1939 and Central High School yearbooks, except the furthest date back was 1953. I also looked in the New Hampshire room in the library," she added.

I looked further. The three John Coughlins in the Manchester phone book were all dead ends. I went through old city directories and got some leads but they went cold. Then I checked in with the alumni office at Trinity High School—they have a lot of the yearbooks from Manchester's old parochial schools—but the only John Coughlin on the books graduated well after the war.

It could be that Ernie Pyle's John Coughlin never went to high school in Manchester or it could be that he never graduated—lots of guys left school to enlist during the war—so for the time being, at least for Erin and me, he exists only in a Pyle dispatch entitled "Night Convoy," filed from Tunisia on Feb. 16, 1943.

Normally, that would be the end of the search, but normally, I'm not working with a kid like Erin Kane—a kid whose curiosity needs to be nourished—so I went off on a parallel tack.

I have my own favorite Ernie Pyle book. It's called "Brave Men." It's a similar compilation of columns and one of them—called "American AckAck"—has been stuck in my mind for a long, long time.

The reason? In writing that piece, Ernie Pyle spent time with two boys from Manchester who were, he noted "so new at war that, they still tried to keep themselves clean." The boys were with the 110th Battery attached to the 1st Army. They were manning a 90-millimeter anti-aircraft gun on Normandy Beach. It was D-Day plus 12 hours and Pyle tried to capture the moment in his simple, understated style.

"Two of the crew were from the same home town," he wrote, "Manchester, New Hampshire. They were Privates Armand Provencher and Jim Bresnahan. In fact there were six Manchester boys in the battery and 15 in the battalion. They all went into the Army on the same day, at the same place and they were firing within a few miles of each other in France."

Pyle was intrigued by Armand Provencher.

"Private Provencher, of French-Canadian extraction, was the only one of our crew who spoke French, so he did all the foraging," he wrote. "His family spoke French in their home back in New Hampshire. I had always heard that the French-Canadian brand of French was unintelligible to real Frenchmen, but Provencher said he didn't have any trouble."

As always, Pyle filled his piece with tiny, telling details; the boredom and the exhaustion, the ten-in-one rations, the singing of sniper bullets, the close quarters of the gun pit, the thrump-thrump sound of distant planes, the flash of guns and the streaking of red tracers far away.

"We never saw the planes we were shooting at," he wrote, "unless it went down in flames, and 'flamers' were rare."

I can't tell you how long it's been since I first read that book, but I always wondered what became of those two soldiers from my home town. Unlike Erin, I had never given in to my curiosity.

On Wednesday, for her sake as much as mine, I did.

First, I picked up the Manchester phone book. I found a James Bresnahan. Then I found an Armand Provencher. Then I picked up the phone and dialed. After so many years, it was too easy.

I caught Jim walking in the door of his house on South Beech Street.

"Oh sure, I remember Ernie Pyle," he said. "Very nice guy. Short guy. Baldish with gray hair. One thing I remember about him, a fella was smoking and he told him to put it out because the Germans could see the light from the cigarette.

"We were young, 18-or-19-year-olds," he added, "and we were just fortunate enough to be where he was those nights."

As for Pyle's story, Jim—who retired in 1985 after spending 32 years with the city's parking meter department—didn't see it for a while.

"I was overseas," he said, "but my parents saw it. There was another person from Manchester by that same name, Jim Bresnahan, and they thought it was about him but it was about me. I still have a letter that Ernie signed for me, but I don't know where it is. It was so long ago."

When I caught up with Armand Provencher, well, I couldn't catch him right away. His wife was busy watching their grandchildren and he was taking a nap—"He's not a young man," his wife said—but he called me later on.

"Oh, Ernie Pyle," he said, "he stayed with us three, four days and he talked to us all from Manchester. There was a Polish guy who died right after the war—I can't remember his name right now—and Jack Bean, he's in Florida. We lost Red Horan and there was Teddy Bobotas, too. Teddy just died last month. Around here, from our unit, there's only me left and Bresnahan."

Armand, now 76, remembered Pyle's fascination with his French.

"It's because I could get a lot of good things from the farmers.

Eggs. Cheese. Liquor. Women," he laughed. "I'm only kidding about the women. But the other stuff, I'd get it for the guys. Not for the whole battery, but enough for my two or three friends and Ernie Pyle, he noticed that."

Both men also took notice of the reason behind my call. They were intrigued by Erin's interest in events from so long ago. "I'm surprised, a young woman like that taking an interest in Ernie Pyle," said Jim, who juggled his schedule for the chance to meet her. Armand was game, too.

They met on Friday. Erin took notes while they talked. Armand told her about being shipped to England aboard the Queen Mary. Jim told her about German soldiers—desperate to surrender—trying to sneak aboard the landing craft after the dust had settled on Normandy Beach. Both men told her about Ernie Pyle.

"Armand got a lot more ink than I did," he explained to Erin, "but that's because I was the quiet one. You know, they had a photographer here at the paper for years named George Naum. He had the same kind of personality as Ernie Pyle. Ernie was a regular guy. Nicest man in the world."

It went like that for a while. They talked. She listened. She asked questions. They answered. She wrote it all down. Just like Ernie Pyle.

For the record, Ernie Pyle was killed by a Japanese sniper on the tiny island of Ie Shima in the spring of 1945. For all of the time that has passed since then, his writing still resonates with a 12-year-old girl named Erin Kane.

Oh, and one more thing. If you bump into Pvt. John Coughlin, tell him that Erin would still like to meet him. I think he'd like to meet her, too.

☆ ☆ ☆

Thanks to a handful of readers, I caught up with someone last week. His name is John Coughlin, and in case you missed last week's column, a brief recap is in order.

A Hillside Middle School student named Erin Kane has been reading a book of columns by legendary war correspondent Ernie Pyle. It's called "Ernie's War." When she came upon a piece Pyle filed on Tunisia in 1943, she noticed that, on page 79, he visited with a Pvt. John Coughlin from Manchester.

What, Erin wondered, ever bacame of him?

This being Manchester, I figured the best thing to do was toss the assignment to my research staff—that's you, by the way—and see what turned up.

John Coughlin turned up.

He's in Gainesville, Fla.

That information came my way from a host of sources. His niece Mary Ann Kowalik called me. His wife's godson, Jay Gagne, called me. His old friend Arthur Normand called me. I even got an e-mail from retired firefighter Dennis Shea—he's down in Margate, Fla.— reminding me that John once owned a corner store in The Flats, a store we visited every single day when we were kids.

Anyway, John Coughlin is 80 now, but Erin, if you're out there, you'll be happy to know that he remembers his drive with Ernie Pyle as if it were yesterday.

"I was a runner," he said. "I was with the 601st Tank Destroyers attached to the 3rd Infantry Division and I was a dispatch runner. I had a motorcycle at one time, but when I seen Ernie Pyle, I had a Jeep.

"I knew who he was," he added. "Hal Boyle was there also from the New York Times. They were with us because it was the closest you could get to the front. The MPs would pull you back unless you had a good reason, like myself, to bring a message from battalion to the infantry commands."

For shepherding such important journalistic cargo through the desert, John won mention in a Pyle column titled "Night Convoy: Feb. 16, 1943." Of course, seeing as how he was in North Africa, John didn't see that column, but Lucille Gagne did.

"I was his fiancée at the time," Lucille said. "Ernie Pyle stories weren't in the newspaper in Manchester, but this person from New York, this good person, she sent it to his mother, so I wrote to thank that lady and she kept on sending us whatever Ernie Pyle wrote. What a nice lady."

And what a nice surprise for the Coughlins, to be remembered by so many folks in their old hometown. After all, he sold Johnny's Corner Store in 1958 and it's been 33 years since John left his job at the VA Hospital in Manchester to take a similar post in Gainesville, where they are now savoring their retirement.

They still get back to town every so often—Easter, most recently— and here's hoping that on their next trip, Pvt. John Coughlin, now a private citizen, will get to meet Citizen Erin Kane.

(5/15/00)

They may have been Prisoners of War on opposite sides of the world, but the strong bond between Gerry Hebert, left, and Arthur "Bud" Locke has been cemented even further by a simple penny postcard. (Union Leader Photo by Bob LaPree)

The Postcard

SOMETIMES A GOOD VETERAN's story can't wait for Veterans Day. This is one of them.

It can't wait because those men and women who make up what Tom Brokaw called "The Greatest Generation" are leaving us in ever-increasing numbers and besides, it isn't every day when you get a guy like Gerry Hebert to talk about his days in a German POW camp.

His wife, Lucille, has never even heard the first part of this story, and Gerry Hebert loves his wife.

"I was a machine gunner," he said. "I didn't want to be a machine gunner. I wanted to join the Navy but they wouldn't take me because I had a steel plate in my arm. The Army didn't care though. They took me."

That was in 1943. After he enlisted, they took him from his parent's home in Hooksett and sent him to basic training in South Carolina. That's where they made him a machine gunner.

"We used to do drills in the tall grass," he said, smiling ever so slightly at the memory. "I was with a rifle patrol. The sergeant would blow a whistle and we were all supposed to dive and take cover in the grass but I was afraid of snakes. He'd blow the whistle and everyone else would be down and I'd still be standing there, looking for a place to fall where there weren't any snakes. That's how I became a machine gunner."

A raised eyebrow gets him talking again.

"That was my punishment," he said. "Every time I wouldn't dive in the grass, I had to spend the night cleaning the machine gun. It got so I could do anything with that gun. Eyes closed. Blindfolded. It didn't matter. I was deathly afraid of snakes, so I spent a lot of time with that machine gun."

It was a 30-caliber, water-cooled machine gun. That's the gun he was manning in Italy. He was with H Company, a heavy weapons unit attached to the 2nd Battalion, 157th Infantry Regiment. The members of that battalion had the misfortune to find themselves at Anzio.

Their ultimate action is a military footnote known as "The Battle of the Caves." After being pounded by German artillery for six days—Gerry still wears a hearing aid in his left ear—the 2nd Battalion had suffered 75 percent casualties.

When the survivors had exhausted their ammunition, 402 men were taken prisoner. Gerry Hebert was among them. It was Feb. 23, 1944.

He wound up in Stalag VII-A, a concentration camp in Moosburg, Germany. As the war raged on and German supplies dwindled, he was shifted to a forced labor unit on a farm in the Bavarian village of Schwabmuehlhausen. It would be more than a year before he would taste freedom again.

"We were liberated on Apr. 27, 1945," he said.

Not that he was heading right home. The Army wanted all former POWs from the European theater sent to a "redistribution center" in Lake Placid, N.Y. He got there in August.

"I think they thought we were all crazy," said Gerry, who weighed all of 80 pounds. "There's one thing when you're in a POW camp, though. You learn how to finagle. I was out of there in eight days."

He was off to Fort Lee, Virginia.

He left Lake Placid so fast, he even missed mail call.

☆ ☆ ☆

Meanwhile, on the other side of the world, another Hooksett native—Arthur "Bud" Locke—was living out his own version of hell.

Bud was a first sergeant with the Far East Air Service Command based in the Philippines. Thus, he was in the wrong place at the wrong time on April 9, 1942, when the Allied forces—out-gunned, out-manned, out-flanked and out of food—were forced to surrender to the Japanese.

"All we had to do was await our fate," he said.

What awaited them was the Bataan Death March.

Bud was one of the lucky ones. He survived the 70-mile trek. An estimated 10,000 Allied troops—American and Filipino—were not so fortunate.

"If there was any hell on earth," he said, "we certainly were in it."

From the steaming, fetid Philippine jungle, he was shipped to a forced labor POW camp in Kobe, a major port on the main Japanese island of Honshu. Things got better, but only by degrees. There was slightly more food—he developed a taste for fish eyes—but the extreme cold rivaled the extreme heat of the Philippines.

"All of us suffered as the real winter arrived," Bud wrote in a memoir entitled "Kobe House POW No. 13." "This made it almost impossible for anyone with pneumonia or the like to ever get well. As a result, during the winter of 1942-43, 120 British died. Two American officers died of pneumonia as well. As cold as we were all the time, it was a wonder more of us didn't wind up dead."

His imprisonment lasted for three-and-a-half years. Even though the Japanese announced their surrender on Aug. 14, 1945, it was more than a month before he finally left Japan, then 10 more days until he reached the train station in Manchester on the way to Hooksett. He took a bus from there.

"Nobody knew I was coming," he said, "and when I walked the quarter mile to our house and knocked on the door, my mother almost had a heart attack. I should have known better. At long last I was home again. . . about 10 years older and 30 pounds lighter. A bit wiser too, I think."

Like many men of their generation, Gerry and Bud put the horrors of World War II behind them and got on with their lives.

The first thing Gerry did when he got home was to marry his sweetheart, Lucille Belisle, the girl he met on the merry-go-round at Pine Island Park. Since then, he put in more than 40 years with the Manchester Water Works, years in which he and Lou raised two kids. Now they have two grandsons.

For Bud, the end of the war meant a continuation of his career in the military. All told, he put in 27 years before coming home to Hooksett where—at the age of 84—he still volunteers in the public library. In his free time, he also volunteers at the Veterans Administration Medical Center.

"I'm a stamp collector, too," Bud said. "I go around to all the shows and look for stamps, and if I see any Hooksett post cards, I buy them. I've been doing that for years, but at my age, I'm starting to get rid of my collection. I started looking through them last month and then I started reading the backs thinking I might know someone. I'd never taken the time to do that before, and geez, I see this one."

Let's let Gerry take over the narrative.

"They have these POW meetings at the VA every month," Gerry said. "I always take a seat on the side so if Bud comes in, he can sit with me. Then I heard someone behind me say, 'Hey, No. 31269313.' Bells started to ring. I thought, 'That's my serial number.' If you're in a POW camp, you never forget your serial number. Then Bud said 'I think this is yours.'"

It was a postcard from Gerry's mother.

It was postmarked Aug. 18, 1945.

You can't blame this belated delivery on the Post Office. Blame Gerry. Had he stayed in Lake Placid long enough, he would have received the card 55 years ago, but Gerry was in a hurry to get on with his life. Now a part of that life—a penny postcard—has finally caught up with him.

On the front, there's a picture of a calm pond below the local landmark known as Pinnacle Rock and the simple legend "Greetings From Hooksett, N.H." On the back is a mother's heartfelt message.

"Dearest son Gerry," she wrote, "So happy to know that everything is all right with you. Have a good time dear, it won't be long before Lou can be with you for always so you can both be happy as you deserve. Will write you a letter tomorrow night. Love luck & kisses, Mom."

Gerry's a quiet guy with an easy smile, but it's a different, tight-lipped smile when he cradles the creased postcard in his open hand.

He won't say it, but at the age of 75, you can tell that postcard probably means more to him than any other keepsake he plans to pass along to his children; more than his Combat Infantry Badge or the Presidential Unit Citation or his European Campaign Medal, even more than his Bronze Star.

"Reading that," he said with that sideways smile, "it's almost like my mother was talking to me again."

(4/24/00)

Of Man and Machine

AT THIS TIME OF YEAR, it's customary for snowbirds to fly south from New Hampshire to Florida to escape the winter weather. Most of them fly back.

Not Bob Carr.

The Dover native made the trip to the Gulf Coast almost 25 years ago and he's still down there. Unlike most snowbirds, though, he does his own flying. It's just that he hasn't got his helicopter pointed up this way yet. And that helicopter? It's the same one he flew 30 years ago.

He wasn't in Florida then.

He was in Vietnam.

Back in March of 1970, Bob Carr was a warrant officer with A Company of the 101st Assault Helicopter Battalion. The unit was part of the 101st Airborne—he was with an outfit known as the Comancheros—and one of his birds was a brand new UH-1H helicopter. It was tagged Chopper 502. Some military folks called it a "slick." Most GIs knew it as a "Huey."

"We flew them from pick-up zones to landing zones for combat assaults," said Bob, whose unit was based in Hue, just south of the DMZ—the so-called Demilitarized Zone—in South Vietnam.

"One day, we did supply missions, the next day we did troop-drops. We did anything they needed. Over there, helicopters were the preferred mode of transportation, in or out. Especially out."

He knows about that last part. The Army made sure of that. Helicopter pilots with the 101st Airborne had to spend their first two weeks in Vietnam on the ground with a rifle.

"They'd take you out in a helicopter and dump you in a field," he said. "They wanted you to know what it was like to be an infantryman, to know what it was like for those men down there on the bottom. It

Dover native Bob Carr has found a perfect fit, with his old Vietnam-era Huey and with the flight suit he wore with the 197th Field Artillery Group of the New Hampshire National Guard. (Photo by Jonathan Fredin/Charlotte Sun Herald)

gave you a real appreciation for what you were going to be doing."

It also gave him a real appreciation for the reliability of his equipment. As any pilot will attest, there's an odd bond that develops between man and machine, but when that machine is the only thing keeping you from a prolonged stay in a POW camp—or a flag-draped coffin—the bond is even stronger.

As if to reinforce the point, Bob's favorite bird was occasionally struck by ground fire—"ventilated" is the term he used—but when it was time for him to come home, Chopper 502 was still flying high.

So was Bob. He signed up as an "air observer" with the 197th Field Artillery Group of the New Hampshire National Guard—"Still proud to be a Minuteman," he noted—which allowed him to continue flying choppers. He even enrolled in East Coast Aero Tech to figure out what made them tick, and the diploma he earned became his ticket to the Sunshine State.

"I got a job in 1975 with the Lee County Mosquito Control Division," he said, (and the simple fact that they need to employ helicopters should give you an indication of the mosquito problems in Lee County, Florida.) "It was a good way for me to keep flying, for one thing, and it was a way to get the mechanical experience I needed, and when a guy crashed one—a small two-seater—I got to rebuild my first helicopter."

It wasn't long before word about Bob, a 1963 graduate of Exeter High School, began to spread throughout Florida.

"The sheriff in Charlotte County heard about my background and he said, 'Guess what? I'm going to get a couple helicopters from the military and I want you to help me get them rebuilt.' I said yes, and in 1978, we started the first aviation program in the sheriff's office. I became a pilot, a mechanic and a Charlotte County deputy sheriff."

The duties there went well beyond mosquitoes.

"With the sheriff's department, we use the helicopters for drug interdiction," he said. "Over the years, the federal government had down-sized its customs and DEA presence in Florida, and they said 'If you locals want to pick up on domestic marijuana eradication. . .' and we slipped right into it."

Funding for the project wasn't exactly flush, however, and if he was going to keep his department's helicopters up in the air, Bob realized he would have to become a scavenger of the highest order.

"Parts is parts," he laughed. "We just put the parts together and away we go. I scan a government web page called DRMO—that's for the Defense Reutilization and Marketing Office—and see what kind of old military property they're offering."

Prowling the Internet on a daily basis, though, got him to thinking.

"I spent so many years trying to forget about Vietnam," he said, "then one day I decided I wanted to know if there was anyone out there on the Internet who belonged to my unit in Vietnam."

There was, naturally, and from that first electronic contact with his one-time crew chief, things began to snowball. More than 250 guys from his unit are now linked via the Internet. A June reunion is planned for Fort Campbell, Kentucky and Bob came up with an idea for arriving in style.

"I just figured, wouldn't it be great if I could find my old Huey I flew over there in Vietnam?" he said. "I thought maybe I could fix it up and put it on display."

The likelihood of finding a 1970 vintage helicopter seemed remote, even after the Vietnam Helicopter Pilots Association came up with a list of the choppers assigned to the Comancheros. Bob persisted though, and when he came across Chopper 502 on a scrap list compiled by the General Services Administration, he made his pitch.

"It was my helicopter," he said. "I had to have it, so I called the GSA and they said, 'You can't have it. The helicopter has been assigned to someone else.'"

The end?

Hardly.

His chopper had been assigned to the Charlotte County Mosquito Control unit. Technically, it was already back in his command.

"Of all the places in the world," he said.

Chopper 502 had been assigned to the scrap heap after a 1998 training flight crash at Fort Rucker, Alabama. In December, the carcass was trucked to the sheriff's hangar at the Charlotte County Airport. In the intervening 60 days, Bob and his friends (volunteer snowbirds included) have been busy patching and repairing and retro-fitting the chopper—at no cost to the state—so it looks the way it did 30 years ago.

And even while he's putting together the pieces of his old helicopter, he's busy doing the same thing with the pieces of his life. First it was the acceptance of his service in Vietnam. Then it was re-embracing his Army buddies. Now it is an on-going reconciliation with his children; a son, Daniel Sullivan and a daughter, Cheryl Lepore, who lives in Penacook.

"He's been really excited about this," said Cheryl. "He's taken us up in the sheriff's department helicopter, but never in a Huey. That would be pretty exciting, especially one that he flew in Vietnam."

Make no mistake. Chopper 502 does not belong to Bob Carr. It belongs to the Charlotte County Sheriff's Department. Still, Bob hopes he can take it for one last spin—bear in mind that odd bond between man and machine—before it's permanently assigned to fire-fighting duties with the Florida Division of Forestry.

"I know of a few people who've got their old aircraft, but they're not flying them," he said. "They're putting them on display at airports or in front of VFW halls, but my ultimate goal? I want to restore it and then I want to fly it to the Comancheros reunion at Fort Campbell this summer. Wouldn't that be something?"

And wouldn't it be something if he were to fly it all the way home?

"It would have to be in the summer," he laughed.

"It's too cold up there."

(2/10/00)

New Hampshire veterans like Paul Morris, at left, know they can get to their appointments at the Veterans Administration Medical Center thanks to drivers like Ray Garland. (Union Leader Photo by Bob LaPree)

A Lift for Veterans

RAY GARLAND HAS A CALENDAR that's different from yours and mine. According to the calendar on the wall of his home in Farmington, today is Veterans Day. Tomorrow too. And the next day, and the day after that.

Apparently, Shirley Magoon has the same kind of calendar.

So does Don Perry.

They are just three of the 44 drivers throughout New Hampshire who make the Voluntary Transportation Network work for veterans in need of medical care.

Since 1988, local chapters of the Disabled American Veterans have directed this volunteer effort, which is coordinated locally by Ray Ritchotte. He's the one at the Veterans Administration Medical Center in Manchester who keeps track of the patients and the drivers and the hours and the miles and pretty soon—they're closing in on the two-million mile mark—he's going to need a new adding machine.

"This year, in the first six months, we did 148,502 miles," he said. "That's an average of 40 riders a day and 1,179 miles per day. In the six months, the volunteers donated 6,606 hours, and if you're looking to put a dollar sign on it, at $13.73 per hour, that's $90,700.38 in value to the VA."

It's worth a lot more than that to the patients.

"They do a great job," said Lou Iacoviello, 82, a former Air Force sergeant from Rollinsford who is scheduled to undergo eye surgery on Oct. 27. "They pick me up at my house and bring me here, then they wait for me and bring me home."

Lou is not just a patient. He's a patient guy. He learned patience after his plane was shot down over Belgium on March 4, 1944. He spent the rest of the war—"It was 14 months and 25 days," he said—in a POW camp in Eastern Prussia.

Lou's rides come through DAV Chapter 4 in Newington, one of 15 chapters in the state that participate in the Voluntary Transportation Network. In each of those chapters, the motto is the same: "The patient comes first."

"You have to remember you're dealing with sick people," said Ray Garland who, at 72, is older than a lot of his passengers. "Sometimes, if someone has a morning appointment and the other guys won't be through until later, we'll make a mid-day run back to Farmington, drop them at home and then go back to Manchester again. You don't want them to sit there all day. You have to put yourself in the veterans' shoes."

Ray can do that. He did a two-year hitch in the Army himself back in the 1940s. But Shirley Magoon? Her empathy comes from a different place.

"I had a husband who was in the Navy and a son who was in the Marines and both of them are deceased," she said, "so I'm just trying to help out where I can."

Where she helps out is in the sprawling parking lots that encircle the VA medical facility. Even those patients who can drive in on their own often face long, pain-filled walks to reach the building, so Shirley constantly runs her shuttle van around the parking lot on Monday mornings.

Close quarters? It would seem so, but she put 5,000 miles on the van last year without ever leaving the parking lot.

Don Perry doesn't have a van. When he leaves his home in Pembroke, he uses his own car—no gas money, no mileage—to get patients to and from the hospital. His motivation?

"I found out I probably get more out of it than the fellas I help," he shrugged. "I guess I just get a satisfaction out of meeting people. Besides, the way I look at it, I got paid back last year."

His payback?

He got to drive another 500 miles.

"A year ago June, they were getting two new vans for the program, and I got picked to go down to Washington and drive one back," he said. "It was one of the best experiences I ever had. There were 149 vans going to 41 different states. They flew us down to Washington and they had a big service on the lawn in front of the Capitol and we got in our vans with flags flying and drove single-file up Pennsylvania Avenue.

"We met up with the folks from Maine and Vermont," he added, "and we convoyed all the way up I-95, all six vans in a row. To me, that ride paid me back for everything."

By the way, the veterans pay nothing for the service people like Don provide. It's all taken care of by the DAV.

"It's plain and simple. If we didn't do this, people wouldn't get here," said Ray Ritchotte. "When you think about the distances—say from Portsmouth to White River Junction in Vermont—a cab ride is out of the question. Even here in Manchester, the average cost of a cab ride for our patients is $12. If you come here three days a week, that adds up fast.

"And if these veterans had to count on their families, it would be a double hit because a lot of family members are working and they'd have to take time off. Like I said, without this program, without all these volunteers, people wouldn't get here, plain and simple."

And if Ray's duties are remarkably complex—scheduling rides for more than 5,000 VA patients around the state—it couldn't be any simpler for the veterans.

"I just pick up the phone," said Paul Morris, who served 25 years with the Special Forces and has 21 knee operations to prove it. "Ray Garland even brought my medication to my house in Rochester after one of my operations. Otherwise I would have gone 11 days without it. He never says no.

"It's a godsend," Paul added. "I can't walk very well and I'm not supposed to drive because of the medication, so three times a week, Ray picks me up and drives me here for my physical therapy. If it wasn't for these guys . . ."

These guys and these gals. They're the ones who make the DAV's Voluntary Transportation Network work. It works because of volunteers like Frank Forest and Roland Hutchins, who got the Farmington DAV to start collecting "Cans for Vans." In the end, Daniel Burrows cashed in 1.5 million cans that paid for a $17,000 van.

It works because of drivers like Ray Garland and Shirley Magoon and Don Perry and Leroy Hunt and Perley Lee and Jim Lazott and so many others who devote so much of their own time to help these veterans.

So why are all these people doing all this work for all these veterans? Don't they know that, with the possible exception of Veterans Day, it has become fashionable to ignore veterans for the rest of the year?

"Apparently," said Ray Ritchotte with a proud smile, "they didn't get that message."

(9/23/99)

Captain Keller

 LIKE OTHER CYNICAL weisenheimers of our time—Groucho Marx and George Carlin come to mind—I had always viewed the phrase "military intelligence" as an hilariously illogical juxtaposition of words—an oxymoron, as it were.

Then I met Amy Keller.

Now I'm confused.

I mean, if our armed forces can muster the intellectual wherewithal to take a brilliant young woman from Manchester and place her in a critical intelligence position in the largest multi-national military coalition since D-Day, how can I pick on them anymore?

As a smart-aleck, it's depressing.

But, as a civic cheerleader of sorts, as a dutiful chronicler of what makes Manchester one of the truly great cities in North America, it is an opportunity to introduce you to a most compelling individual.

Naturally, she's from the West Side—with an educational vitae that includes Parker-Varney, Parkside and the Derryfield School—but to tell her story, we have to do more than cross the Merrimack. We also have to cross the Atlantic, the Mediterranean and the Red Sea, too—eight time zones in all if you're resetting your watch—until we touch down in Saudi Arabia.

That's where Capt. Amy Keller served with the U.S. Air Force during Operation Desert Shield as a member of the 9th Tactical Intelligence Squadron, a unit whose SAT scores, I can assure you, will never, ever, be confused with those of the Board of Mayor and Aldermen.

Her role in Desert Shield and its offspring, Operation Desert Storm, was to provide daily intelligence briefings to Lt. Gen. Charles Horner, the man who directed the air war over Iraq (and in case you've forgotten, the lion's share of the war was conducted in the not-so-friendly skies above Baghdad.)

Her blonde hair made her stand out in Saudi Arabia, but Captain Amy Keller (USAF) has always been a standout in her hometown. (Photo Courtesy of Mr. and Mrs. Bruce Keller)

"I was working with a stable of analysts that was broken into units, and after the different units would brief me, I would meet with Gen. Horner and update him on what the bad guys were doing," said Amy, a 1987 Dartmouth graduate.

"That was a kind of a glamour job," she admitted, since a big guy by the name of Schwarzkopf would occasionally sit in, "but later on, I was shifted to the Tactical Electronic Order of Battle.'"

Sounds like a great Nintendo game, but in that role, Amy helped pinpoint Iraqi radar and surface-to-air missile sites and communicate that data to the pilots.

"We had to find those sites to take out their eyes and ears," she said. "While people in the States were hearing so much about Scuds, we were more concerned with missiles that could take out our aircraft. As we saw it, there were pilots with families back home that were depending on us. Whenever we'd start getting tired, we'd remind one another of that fact to keep going."

When she wasn't working—everybody drew 14-hour shifts, seven days a week—she was living on the outskirts of Riyadh in Eskan Village, a condo complex that had been abandoned by Bedouins.

"When we first arrived in August of 1990, the Saudi government was putting us up in four and five-star hotels," she said. "Eventually, we were moved out of the city to minimize the terrorist threat, but that's not the only reason. King Fahd had told Gen. Horner that our being there, the women in particular, was a bigger threat to Saudi Arabia than the Iraqis."

Hardly a warm welcome, but Amy—who had prepared for her Middle East duty with laugh-a-minute courses like Dynamics of International Terrorism—was sensitive to the cultural differences.

"They're very proud of their lifestyle, much of which is dictated by the Koran, and they believe their culture is one from which we Americans can learn a great deal," she said.

Like how to wear an "abbaya" the shapeless black garment favored by Arabic women who wish to avoid confrontations with the religious police, known as "muttawa." Think of them as the Moral Majority in turbans.

"By wearing the abbaya when we were off duty, we were able to erase a lot of our sexuality, which was important. Even a shirt tucked in at the waist was considered sexy there, so we bought our own abbayas. It's hard to explain, but not wearing one would have been like walking down the street naked.

"A lot of the American women even carried veils," she added. "If you were walking down the street without one, the muttawa would come over and start tapping his cane at your feet until you covered your hair."

In Amy's case, it's shoulder-length blonde hair, as rare in the Arab world as were her blue eyes, but in spite of immersion in a foreign culture, with a war so close at hand, she says she never felt less concern for her personal safety.

"It's the safest place I've ever seen," she said. "People would look at us, but no one would ever touch us, and if you went into one of the gold shops and they didn't have what you wanted, the owner would simply walk out and take you to another shop without even locking his door. No one steals."

And with good reason. There are serious deterrents to crime in Saudi Arabia.

If you steal, they cut off your hand. If you kill, they cut off your head, and if you commit a sexual assault? Let's just say that the punishment for sexual assault would make ritual circumcision seem like a gentle, loving caress, if you get my drift.

The venue for this justice system—there is no appellate court, by the way—is "Chop-Chop Square." That's what the Americans called the executioner's block in downtown Riyadh. Amy avoided it.

"They didn't have any problem with Westerners coming to see what they do," she said, "but I didn't feel the need to see something like that. We were working under life and death circumstances anyway. That was enough."

So was eight months of duty in Saudi Arabia.

Thus, when her four-year hitch with the Air Force expired shortly after her return to the States, Amy returned to Manchester. Surprising? Not when you realize that her family has been here for eight generations.

Her father, Bruce Keller, is a vice president with the Kalwall Corp., and her mother, Cynthia Keller, is a member of the Elliot Hospital board of trustees, and now Amy is settling down back into her hometown.

While she is busy with her two daughters, her duty with the Air National Guard and her career (as VP of a start-up venture called Ocean Vision Technology,) she's also found time for volunteer work with Habitat for Humanity.

"I had a lot of good friends over there who were refugees, and seeing people without homes really stays with you," said Amy, whose return to Manchester can only benefit the city that we call home.

(11/30/92)

Dec. 7, 1941

 IT WAS WEDNESDAY, Dec. 3, 1941. A Marine Corps sergeant named Walter Welch took advantage of a day's liberty and left his ship—the U.S.S. San Francisco—to go visit a buddy from Manchester.

His name was Joe Rozmus. He was a sailor whose ship was anchored just across the bay in Pearl Harbor.

"We made plans to go to Waikiki Beach on Sunday," he said.

They never made it.

Instead of a day at the beach, Welch and his comrades endured a day in hell. At 7:45 that Sunday morning, he was leading a color guard onto the fantail of the San Francisco when the first Japanese planes were spotted.

When the day was over, President Roosevelt called it "a date which will live in infamy." For Walter Welch, it was the date he watched his friend's ship—the U.S.S. Arizona—destroyed by Japanese bombs.

"I'll never forget it as long as I live," he said. "I was standing aft and I saw it get hit. The explosions were horrible. I saw men and debris flying through the air and I saw it break in half. There's a fellow from Manchester who lives in Merrimack now, Bob Lefabvre. He was on the deck of the West Virginia and the blast from the Arizona blew him right off his ship."

Joe Rozmus died that day. So did 1,176 others aboard the Arizona. All told, 2,403 died—including others from Manchester like Seaman 1st Class David Crossett and Pfc. Peter Gravas and Sgt. Maurice St. Germain and Pvt. Joseph Jedrysik—in the attack that occurred 54 years ago today.

Those men will be among those remembered today at 10 a.m. during a memorial gathering at the State House in Concord. At the same time, special license plates will be presented to men like Walter Welch

Pearl Harbor survivor Walter Welch could never forget the sense of help-lessness that marked his experience in Hawaii on Dec. 7, 1941. (Union Leader Photo by George Naum)

and Bob Lefabvre, members of the New Hampshire chapter of the Pearl Harbor Survivors Association. While the group has 63 known members, only 25 are expected to attend the services.

Even heroes are not exempt from the ravages of time.

Time normally takes its toll on memories as well, but sometimes the memories of that Sunday morning on Pearl remain all too vivid for the survivors.

"It's not too bad when people ask direct questions, like 'What kind of ship was the Arizona?' or 'How many people were killed?'" said Welch. "It's when they ask you what you were feeling that day. That's when the memories start to get the better of you."

Even after 54 years.

Perhaps it's because the memories involve anger and rage. Most of all, those memories involve frustration.

"We were Marines, but we weren't sea-going bellhops on board ship," he said. "We manned 5-inch anti-aircraft guns. Mine was on the port side and we were trained to fire four shells in 16 seconds and we could hit a target as far as 3,200 yards away."

All of that training flashed through his mind when he saw those first planes—maybe a dozen of them—swoop over Hickam Field and make their way toward battleship row. He saw the insignia of the Rising Sun and he heard the loudspeaker bark to life: "The island of Oahu is under attack—all men to battle stations!"

On board the San Francisco, it was a futile command.

"We were supposed to go into dry dock for overhaul on Monday," Welch said. "We had to make the ship lighter. Two days earlier, we had unloaded our turret ammunition and our anti-aircraft shells. Three thousand rounds."

Knowing their big guns had been rendered useless, Welch led his four-man detail below deck where they were able to grab four Browning automatic rifles. They hefted boxes of ammo, bolted topside and started firing at the bombers overhead. The memory makes Welch shake his head.

"Firing at a bomber with a BAR," he says softly before looking away.

Those are the memories that hit him the hardest, the ones that bring back the sense of helplessness he felt that day. For all of the personal pain, however, it's a memory he keeps alive. It's a memory he shares with youngsters when he visits schools here in his hometown of Manchester.

To help the kids understand what happened that day, this most meticulous man has a carefully prepared set of diagrams. Even at 80, his military bearing and banking background are still evident. He has a time line and photographs and maps to share but, the most important part of his presentation—the part that brings Pearl Harbor to life for these kids—is the story they hear from this eyewitness to history.

More than the charts, it's what's in his heart.

Even after 54 years.

(12/7/95)

The price of battle, while steep, can be matched by the price of eternal vigilance, as the family of Major Robert Plamondon would discover. (Photo Courtesy of Irene Plamondon Swist)

The Last Full Measure of Devotion

FROM ITS VERY INCEPTION, the notion of Memorial Day was to honor America's war dead, but what of those men and women who, in the words of Abraham Lincoln, "gave the last full measure of devotion" outside the field of battle?

What of men like Major Robert Plamondon? Was his sacrifice somehow less supreme?

☆ ☆ ☆

There was little doubt about Bob Plamondon's career plans when he was graduated from Central High School in 1948.

"He was so patriotic," said Irene Plamondon Swist. "He joined right out of high school as soon as he could. He just wanted to serve his country and was definitely meant for the service. He loved it. He absolutely loved it.

"He polished his brass every single day. He spit polished his shoes every single day. He had a lot of pride and he had even more when he put on that uniform."

It was the uniform of the New Hampshire National Guard.

It was the uniform of the 195th Infantry.

He didn't wear it long.

"We were married on Aug. 18, 1951, at Sacred Heart Church," Irene said, "and just before we were married, he put in for officer candidate school. He wanted to be an Army pilot. We had to switch uniforms."

Military wives do that. They use the collective "we" because if the husband switches uniforms, so does the wife. If the husband is promoted, so is the wife. If the husband is transferred, so is the wife. Irene was transferred 31 times.

"When he went to officer candidate school at Fort Benning, I couldn't go with him right away," she said, "but after a couple of months, he found me a room. I couldn't live with him, but I could be near him."

Eventually, the kids could be near him, too.

Bob Jr. was born when he was at Camp Breckenridge in Kentucky. Susan was born—amazingly enough—when he was right here in Manchester. Marc was born when he was at Cigli Air Base in Izmir, Turkey.

That was in 1964.

The family couldn't follow him to his next assignment.

When Bob Plamondon arrived in Vietnam in 1965, he was doing double duty. He was assigned to an artillery unit and he was also manning the stick of a UH-1D gunship—the ubiquitous Huey—with the 162nd Assault Helicopter Company.

Helicopter or fixed-wing? It didn't matter to Major Plamondon. If it flew, he could fly it. He was qualified for every piece of aircraft in the Army hangar, but it was in his chopper that he would fly highest.

He was in that chopper on April 29, 1966.

He had already been in the air for 12 hours that day, yet he volunteered to make night flights into Tay Ninh Province. Two infantry battalions were trapped and their critical supplies—water, food and ammunition—were all but gone.

"He dauntlessly flew into the rendezvous area," one citation reads, "which had not been secured from the threat of Viet Cong attack, to ensure coordination with ground forces before supply flights began."

However, in the ink-black night of the Asian jungle, the ground troops couldn't locate the landing zone, so Major Plamondon, "using the sound of his engines," guided them to the site. He put down through a narrow opening in the trees.

"For two hours, he guided pilots into the hazardous landing zone, using only a dim flashing light and radioed instructions to keep them clear of obstacles in the dark. Through his selfless efforts, the supply missions were flown without accident and the material strength of the ground units was restored."

All told, he flew 175 missions in Vietnam, but that one on April 29, 1966, won him the Distinguished Flying Cross. A month later, he won the Bronze Star, but when you ask Irene Plamondon Swist about that one, she just looks at you, palms up.

"I went to so many of those ceremonies," she apologized. "It must be my old brain, but I just can't remember which one was for what anymore."

After his two tours in Vietnam, Bob Plamondon was reunited with his family. He was assigned to Hanau, Germany. He was made commanding officer of the 122nd Aviation Company, which conducted aerial surveillance. The plane of choice was the Grumman OV-1 Mohawk, a turbo-prop plane used to photograph surrounding terrain.

Among the Mohawk's nicknames? "The Widowmaker."

The Army decided to consolidate its fleet under Major Plamondon's command. Every Mohawk on every U.S. base in Europe was to be retrieved and returned to Hanau. Eventually, only one remained. It was in Italy. Someone had to go get it and fly it back. It was Oct. 12, 1967. Columbus Day. It's not a holiday in Germany, but it was for the U.S. military personnel at Hanau.

"That's why Bob took the flight," Irene said. "It was a holiday and being the commander, he didn't want to give it to one of the other guys. He was a good boss, so he took the turn."

He took the turn with his second in command, Major Robert Jenkins. Two men. Fly out together on one plane—a Mohawk—and fly back separately in two planes.

"He had left really early that morning, about 4 o'clock," Irene said. "He woke me up. He laughed. He said, 'Do you have any money?' It was very difficult to cash a check over there. You had to stand in line at the American Express and they'd only give you 25 dollars at a time but he had such a grin I always gave in.

"I told him to take the cash. He said, 'You know what? Make reservations in Augsburg.' It was a Thursday. He said, 'I'll be back Saturday. We'll go out to dinner. Later that day, I looked out the window and I saw Father (John) Russell. He was from Blessed Sacrament right here in Manchester and he was over there with us. He was coming toward the house. . ."

The Mohawk had crashed near Bologna, Italy.

The cause: mechanical failure.

Irene Plamondon was flown home, with her three children, in the first class compartment of a DC-10. Ten days later, her husband's body came home. He was buried in Mount Calvary Cemetery.

Irene has not forgotten those details.

Those, you never forget.

Today, we observe a holiday so we may never forget.

"On Memorial Day, I feel for everybody," Irene said, "but the anniversary of Bob's death probably means more to me. I think of him all the time, but on his birthday and the anniversary of his death—it always falls on a holiday—it hits you more. You have the whole day to think about it."

We have a whole day to think about it today.

We have a whole day to think about how the price of battle, while steep, can be matched by the price of eternal vigilance. Bob Plamondon paid that price.

He—and others like him—should also be remembered today.

(5/28/01)

The Chosin Few

WHEN HAROLD BERLIND was a child, he envisioned hell as a place of eternal fire and flame.

In 1950, the U.S. Marine from Dover found out he was wrong.

Hell was cold, bitter cold. Hell was mountainous terrain covered in gritty snow. Hell was filled with waves and waves of attacking Chinese soldiers.

Hell was right here on Earth, in Korea, at the Chosin Reservoir.

In the 40 years since the epic retreat from Chosin, the Korean War has become an increasingly hazy memory in the minds of the American people, prompting veterans to dub the three-year conflict "The Forgotten War."

It has not been forgotten by the men who fought there, many of whom are now members of a fraternal veterans organization known as "The Chosin Few."

Nor has it been forgotten by Groveton native Michael Moffett, a Marine reservist who hopes to use New Hampshire's rugged North Country landscape as the setting for a film about a U. S. military defeat that some historians have labeled the most savage battle in modern warfare.

Moffett wasn't born until five years after the battle at Chosin but his fascination with military history and his own 1984 tour of duty in Korea have spawned a film project that is gaining momentum.

"Essentially, the battle at Chosin contained all the worst elements of Valley Forge, the Alamo and Custer's Last Stand, all American military disasters, only in this case there were 15,000 men at risk," said Moffett. "The way they managed to fight their way out, while also fighting the fierce North Korean winter, may be the greatest feat of American arms ever accomplished."

At the end of the month, The Chosin Few will reunite in Las Vegas

Marine Corps Reserve Capt. Michael Moffett of Groveton served in Operation Desert Storm, but it's another heroic Marine Corps action—at the Chosin Reservoir in Korea—that he wants people to remember. (Photo Courtesy of Nancy Moffett)

to commemorate the battle that has been likened to an American Dunkirk, yet in the proud history of the U.S. Marines, Chosin is remembered not as a rout, not as a retreat, but as a victory.

To be sure, other branches of the service were there. Retired Army Major Gerald J. Clinton of Rye will attest to that. So will Robert Sambataro of Hampton, a retired Navy petty officer.

But Chosin is remembered as a Marine battle, a story of heroism and suffering made all the more poignant by the staggering odds the Marines defied and the flipness with which they defied them.

"Retreat hell. We're just attacking in a different direction," said Gen. Oliver P. Smith. Another Marine leader, Col. Lewis "Chesty" Puller—the most decorated Marine in Corps history—upon learning that the 15,000-man United Nations force was surrounded by 120,000 Chinese troops, said, "Those poor bastards. We've got them right where we want them. We can shoot in every direction now."

A realistic view generated less cause for optimism.

Against the advice of U.S. intelligence experts, Gen. Douglas MacArthur sent his UN troops into North Korea on a bold offensive foray designed to end the war as swiftly as possible.

Although advance battalions actually reached the banks of the Yalu River on the Chinese border, other senior U.S. officers questioned such a major offensive over such treacherous terrain during the harsh Korean winter.

They also questioned MacArthur's blindness to the rising presence of Chinese Communist forces, and on Nov. 27, 1950, their worst fears were realized.

Waves of Chinese troops descended upon the 5th and 7th Marine encampments on the Chosin Reservoir at Yudam-ni. For five days, they slugged it out with the Chinese in temperatures that dipped to 20-below zero.

Berlind, then a 19-year-old communications specialist, was there.

"We had to keep the lines of communication open, but the enemy would cut the lines and then sit there and wait for someone to come along and fix it," he said. "You'd have to go out at two or three in the morning with a couple riflemen to protect you, so there was a pretty high casualty rate."

When Berlind's unit wasn't battling the enemy, it was battling the elements.

"I've never been so cold in my entire life," he said. "We weren't really dressed for the cold weather except for field jackets and long underwear. You just got so cold you didn't care whether you lived or died."

Hundreds did die, succumbing to the cold and the endless waves of Chinese attackers, whose mission was to annihilate the Marines.

When the odds facing the American troops became apparent, a breakout move was organized. The goal was Hungnam Harbor on the Sea of Japan 78 miles to the south, but the only way to reach it was via a winding, mountain road that was designed as a supply route. In the days ahead, it would become an escape route.

The fragmented Marine units would link up and make their way south via Hagaru, Koto-ri, Chinhung-ni and Hamhung, but the saturation presence of the Chinese ensured it would be a bloody journey.

The first stage of the breakout was Hagaru, site of a tiny airstrip used to evacuate 5,400 of the wounded. The airstrip was defended by a makeshift force of British marine commandos, U.S. soldiers and Marines.

Despite the sub-zero cold, machine gun barrels glowed red hot from constant use. On one charge, bugles and whistles would announce the Chinese assaults. On other occasions, the assaults were made in deadly silence.

The Marine units would launch flares and ignite five-gallon gasoline cans to illuminate their front lines. They would even torch small farmhouses in an effort to light the battlefield, but to little avail.

"It got so we would put out anything we could about 25 yards away from our line—trip-wires, grenades, anything to tip off their attack, but people can get pretty close under cover of darkness," said Lt. Col. Wayne Hall of Hanover, who directed a Marine rifle platoon at Hagaru.

Like most officers, Hall was equipped with a side arm and carbine, but the extreme cold negated the weapon's effectiveness.

"The carbine springs were so cold they just wouldn't eject spent shells, so, you'd have to rip your glove off and pull the shell out by hand, which took about 10 seconds. Plus it just didn't have enough firepower."

Hall found that out the hard way.

"During one assault, I looked up and saw this guy straddling one of our machine guns about 20 feet away from me, so I shot the guy, but he got up for a minute. I went over later and he had a bullet right in the middle of his forehead. That's when I decided to use my .45."

Hall later used the .45 to shoot two other Chinese attackers, in spite of shrapnel wounds to his arm and chest that would earn him a Purple Heart. When he was taken to the aid tent, the thermometer read 37-below. His conduct earned him the Bronze Star.

More importantly, he was able to resume command of his platoon—at Chosin, you weren't considered wounded unless you couldn't fire a rifle. He joined the march southward.

"As we had moved up the land road on the way into Hagaru, we sent people up into the hills and ridges along the road and found nothing," said Hall, "but on the way back, every rock and ridge was hiding someone, and they were shooting at us from every side."

Still, the Marine column advanced steadily down the one-lane, snow-covered road, aided by pilots who roared through the narrow mountain passages to provide air support. The dead and wounded were piled onto trucks, while the able-bodied shuffled along the roadway, confronting the enemy at every turn.

It took 38 hours of fierce fighting and 650 casualties to travel the 11 miles to Koto-ri, where Lt. Gerald J. Clinton of Rye began to feel the effects of frostbite.

"I fought in World War II and jumped on Corregidor when we fought to take it back, and that was a piece of cake compared to what happened at Chosin," said Clinton, who served as Army liaison to the legendary Chesty Puller.

After one firefight, Clinton and another soldier stumbled upon a group of Chinese soldiers and were taken prisoner. They managed to escape from the farmhouse where they were being held, only to be recaptured soon after.

"There was a Chinese behind every tree," he said, "but they were too intent on attacking to bother with prisoners. This time they took us to the end of the perimeter, knee-deep in snow, pointed us toward our lines and said 'walk.'

"I admit I was pretty puckered, expecting to be shot in the back and all, but the only ones who shot at us were the Marines. They couldn't tell who we were because of the poor visibility.

"We were lucky the Chinese were so humane to us, because the North Koreans committed some horrible atrocities," Clinton said. "They would pour gasoline on a truck full of wounded, set it on fire and push it off the mountain."

The mountain road took its own toll, as trucks would skid out of control and veer off the steep cliffs, killing all on board. Still, the procession advanced past Koto-ri until a gaping 1,500-foot deep chasm halted the march. The Chinese had dynamited the lone bridge, prompting an unforgettable example of ingenuity under fire.

Using improvised parachute drops, C-119 Flying Boxcars dropped eight two-ton Treadway bridge sections to the troops from a height of 800 feet. With Marine patrols fending off Chinese assaults, the engineers assembled the units only to come up seven feet short of completion.

Their solution was grisly. A timber frame was assembled at the far end of the bridge and bulldozers filled the gap to road level. When they ran out of loose rock for fill, they used the frozen corpses of the Chinese dead. The march resumed and gathered momentum toward Chinhung-ni.

A relief corps moving north from Hungnam linked up with the troops heading for the safety of the coastal plain, but by then, the Chinese force was weakening.

By the hundreds, Chinese soldiers with frozen hands and feet came down from the hills begging to surrender. Others looked on from the distance, too cold and spent to mount an attack on the Marine column.

In Hungnam harbor, a fleet of 100 American, Japanese and Norwegian ships awaited the 14,000 weary fighting men and thousands of Korean refugees. Lt. Robert Sambataro of Hampton was a medical officer on board the USS Missouri.

"It was so cold that when you wanted to give someone an injection, you had to hold the syringe in your mouth enough to warm it up before you could give them a shot," he said.

Seventeen Chosin combatants were awarded the Congressional Medal of Honor. Seventy more won Navy Crosses, and countless others were cited for their bravery, the most ever for a single battle in US military history.

(11/11/90)

The Fightin' Fifth

MAJOR OTIS WAITE inadvertently issued a challenge to historians back in 1886. The challenge came in a passage from his book entitled "New Hampshire in the Great Rebellion." That's where Waite made the following proclamation:

"May a grateful country do the Fifth New Hampshire Regiment of Volunteers justice—written history never can."

Mark Travis and Mike Pride tried.

In their written history of the Civil War regiment known as the Fighting Fifth, they have tried to do justice to the farm boys and machinists and teachers and mill-hands and shoe-makers from the Granite State who, in their efforts to preserve the Union, suffered more combat deaths than any other unit in the Union Army.

The commander of that unit, Col. Edward Ephraim Cross, referred to his men as "my brave boys." Tomorrow, Cross and those boys will be remembered.

It is in Lancaster where Cross was born and it is in Lancaster where Cross was buried—long after he was felled by a rebel sniper at Gettysburg—and fittingly, it is in Lancaster where Cross and his brave boys will be remembered in story and in song.

The stories will come from Travis and Pride.

The songs will come from the 2nd New Hampshire Regiment Serenade Band, an ensemble that features both music and costumes from the era of the Civil War. That era will also be brought to life by re-enactors from the Fifth Regiment, New Hampshire Volunteer Infantry, who will turn the Weeks Memorial Library into a bivouac for the Army of the Potomac.

"We call it a living history," said Jim Blake, who will make the drive from his Bedford home for the event. "We want to give people a flavor of what a Civil War camp was like. We have all the equipment, the full

Lancaster native Colonel Edward Ephraim Cross and the Fifth New Hampshire Regiment of Volunteers are the basis of the book entitled "My Brave Boys." (Union Leader Photo by Bob LaPree)

uniforms and all the accouterments, from the cartridge belts and cap boxes to the muskets and the haversacks."

Hardtack, too.

"That was a staple of their diet," he said. "It was flour, water and salt. It was in the shape of a Pop Tart, only thicker. Harder, too, but it filled the gap."

For a century, there were annoying gaps in the history of the Fighting Fifth, holes and empty spaces that frustrated scholars and researchers. The greatest void? A journal kept by Col. Cross disappeared at the turn of the last century, and if not for some dogged detective work, a few surreptitious meetings and some financial finagling by Boscawen historian Walter Holden, it might never have resurfaced.

It did. That was in 1965. Even with the journal, however, Holden's efforts to produce a book about the Fighting Fifth stalled.

"It was turned down by a distinguished list of publishers," he laughed.

Thus, when he heard that Travis and Pride were engaged in a similar effort, he offered encouragement. That, and the journal of Col. Cross.

"Cross was simply the outstanding hero of New Hampshire in the Civil War," Holden said. "Most Civil War regiments were drawn from specific areas—the Sixth was from the Keene area, for instance—but when Cross chose his 10 captains, he chose one from each of the 10 counties in New Hampshire. It was his outfit all the way."

And his outfit frequently went into harm's way.

There were bloody engagements at Bull Run and Antietam and Fair Oaks and Cold Harbor and Malvern Hill and Fredericksburg and Chancellorsville, among others.

"At the end of the Battle of Gettysburg—and this was only 14 months after they got started—they had less than 100 men of the 1,100 they started with," Holden said. "Some were wounded, others taken by disease. They lost 265 dead, but the men were proud of the figure because they all occurred in hard, stand-up fighting."

Cross was among that number.

He seemed to know when his number was up.

The colonel was famed for wearing a red bandanna into battle. At Gettysburg, he wore black. Here's how Travis and Pride describe the moment in their book, which is entitled "My Brave Boys":

"Given Cross's fatalism on the way to battle. . . (Lt. Charles) Hale found the colonel's new choice of color appalling. Ever dramatic, Cross fussed with his headgear. 'Please tie it tighter, Mr. Hale,' he said. Hands, trembling, Hale obliged. 'Draw it tighter,' the colonel insisted again. Again Hale complied.

"The smoke was now thick and the noise tremendous along Sickle's line. (Gen. Winfield Scott) Hancock approached for a look, his staff trailing. The general reined in his horse at Cross's side, ready with words of encouragement. 'Colonel Cross,' he said, 'this day will bring you a star. Cross shook his head. 'No general,' he said, 'this is my last battle.'"

Shortly thereafter, he was in the sights of a rebel sniper.

He was gut shot; "a mortal wound, and a painful one."

In the hands of a Hollywood screenwriter, that would be the stuff of legend, but truth be told, Cross is accorded something less than legendary status in Lancaster.

"His name isn't exactly on everyone's lips," said Gene Ehlert, the managing editor of the Coos County Democrat, which is the same newspaper where Cross began his career in journalism—pre-Civil War—at the age of 15.

"Frankly, Cross hasn't really won a lot of general play in town and that's why the new book is so interesting," he added. "He will really be getting some recognition now, and for someone like Faith Kent, someone who has direct ties to him, this has to be very gratifying."

At the age of 86, Faith Kent has long been the keeper of the Cross flame. Her grandfather, Henry Kent, was Cross's best friend. The two men corresponded regularly, and when Faith discovered 70 letters in the family home—letters written in Cross's own hand—the archive of the Fighting Fifth was further enriched.

She has been eager to spread the gospel, but.. .

"Over the years, maybe a dozen people have corresponded or telephoned or come in person to talk to me about Col. Cross," she said. "At least three or four of them wrote books, but none of them was ever published. That's why I'm so glad this new one was published."

Her joy is shared by the authors, with whom she shared her letters.

"No historian had ever seen those letters, and for amateur historians like us, that kind of find is like gold," said Pride, who is the editor of The Concord Monitor. His co-author is editorial page director at the same newspaper and for the past eight years, when they weren't working at the paper, they were working on their book.

"This is something that started as a hobby," Travis said. 'We dove in early, found what was easy to find and then we faltered. If we hadn't been working on it together, we might never have gotten it done.

"As journalists," he said, "I think we were prepared for the reporting side of it. A book is something else altogether, but at some point we realized, jeez, this is a great story and it's a story not enough people know about. We can't put it away. We owe it to others to finish it."

They did, and before they're finished tomorrow—the program will run from 1 to 4 p.m.—even more people will know the story of Col. Cross and the Fighting Fifth.

"As we did the research for the book," Pride explained, "one of the things we found is that, while many people view the Civil War as something that happened in Maryland and Virginia, it really happened here. It happened in New Hampshire. It was a huge, transforming event for this state. That's what we'd like people to take away."

(4/21/01)

Shipmates Marcel Pinard, left, and Bernie Lee were on board the USS Quincy when the heavy cruiser secretly transported President Franklin D. Roosevelt to the Yalta Conference. (Union Leader Photo by David Burroughs)

Witness to History

 EVERY DAY IN 1995, it seems, we note an anniversary. We don't celebrate them, we note them, because one does not celebrate anniversaries of war.

Still, when the world was at war 50 years ago, events of global significance were taking place on a daily basis, and now, half a century later, we look back and try to place those events in perspective.

That's what Marcel Pinard and Bernie Lee are trying to do.

Fifty years ago last week, while Allied troops were battling their way toward Berlin and American Marines were planting the flag atop Mt. Suribachi on Iwo Jima, Pinard and Lee were sailors aboard the U.S.S. Quincy, a heavy cruiser that had just knifed its way through the Straits of Gibraltar.

Their cargo?

Franklin Delano Roosevelt.

The President of the United States was on board, en route to a conference in the Crimean resort of Yalta where the fate of postwar Europe would be determined, and two teenagers from Manchester— unknown to one another—were witnesses to history.

It wouldn't be the only time. From the day she left the Fore River shipyard in Quincy, Mass. in 1942, the U.S.S. Quincy was never far from the fray. Her crew was the first to be fired upon during the invasion of Normandy on D-Day, and a year later, they were half a world away, firing her eight-inch guns on Tokyo in the final assault on Japan leading to V-J Day.

"That's why the Crimea mission seemed like a piece of cake in comparison," said Lee, 68, a graduate of the Ash Street School in Manchester who now makes his home in Auburn. "We knew something big was up though, because when we got back from France, we put in at Norfolk, Va., and they started installing an elevator on the ship."

The elevator was for Roosevelt, whose polio-related infirmity was largely unknown to the American public at the time, and the secrecy that shrouded his condition was not unlike the secrecy that permeated the Quincy's mission.

There were other upgrades too, like a bathtub and carpeting and lamps in the captain's quarters that prompted the men to dub the ship "Showboat" in honor of the Broadway show. Before, long, they were Broadway bound themselves.

"We were ordered to New York for the Christmas and New Year's holidays," said Pinard, now 69, "and we thought it was so we could all have shore leave, but then we were restricted to the ship. On starboard watch, you could hear the Christmas songs coming out of New York City."

On Jan. 23, 1945, with Roosevelt on board, they weighed anchor under heavy guard, and their convoy set out. Their destination was the Mediterranean island of Malta and their voyage took them across the Atlantic and through the Straits of Gibraltar where their destroyer escort was on highest alert.

"They called the place 'Torpedo Junction' because so many ships went down there," Lee said. "We were only rated to 21 knots but we were flat out. We had to be doing 24 knots. We were running so fast the bolts were shaking."

Throughout the war, the Quincy's log read like a World War II "who's who." There were your rank and file admirals and generals and field marshalls on board at one time or another, and there was Supreme Allied Commander Dwight D. Eisenhower, who personally informed the crew of their role in the Normandy invasion.

But on this voyage, from the moment they made port at Malta, every day in dock was a lesson in diplomacy as the vessel played host to Roosevelt's visitors.

There were diplomats like Anthony Eden and W. Averell Harriman and then there was British Prime Minister Winston Churchill, whose trademark "V" for victory sign drew cheers from the crew as he marched up the gangplank.

There was royalty too, like Ethiopian Emperor Haile Selassie, Egypt's King Farouk and King Ibn Saud of Arabia, whose entourage of 47 included his fortune teller, his food taster, his royal purse bearer, 10 guards with sabers and daggers and "nine miscellaneous slaves, cooks, porters and scullions."

"And they brought 10 sheep with them for the King, and they

slaughtered them right on the fantail," Pinard said. "They could only eat fresh meat."

In short, it was a perspective on a spectacle that historians could only dream about, and as the years have passed, the significance has grown in their minds.

"With all that was going on in the world, it's hard to imagine now that we were so close to the situation," Pinard said.

"Heck we were just kids," Lee added. "They didn't impress the enormity of it upon us, so for some guys, it was like a pleasure cruise. Once we got through though, I thought that meant the war was over. I was wrong."

He was wrong. Within six months, they were bombing the Japanese and when they were suddenly ordered away from the coast of Nagasaki in August of 1945, they had no idea how the world was about to change.

That's another anniversary to be noted later in the year, however. Meanwhile, Pinard and Lee have some catching up to do.

"I'm proud to have been there with him," Lee said with a nod toward Pinard, "even though we never met until this week."

(2/18/95)

Colonel Perry Lamy of Manchester is flying high in his post as commander of the Air Force Flight Test Center at historic Edwards Air Force Base. (Photo Courtesy of U.S. Air Force)

New Hampshire's "Top Gun"

To ME, when it comes to Edwards Air Force Base, it's all about perspective.

You tell me that folk hero and flying legend Chuck Yeager first broke the sound barrier there back in 1947? Okay. You tell me that Space Shuttle flights routinely land at Edwards? If you say so. And you say that Steve Austin, television's fictional "Six Million Dollar Man" was based there as well? Well, well, well.

You could even point out that the sprawling air base in the California desert was the location of one of the most acclaimed UFO sightings in history—it was Oct. 7, 1965—and the best you'll get from me is mild, feigned interest.

However, you tell me that my West High School classmate—Manchester's own Perry Lamy—is now in command of the 412th Test Wing, which is arguably the most important aviation and flight testing operation in the western World?

You have my undivided attention.

And would you please stand at attention for the general.

"I'm not a general yet," he laughed. "The President nominated me and Congress approved it, but it won't be official until February or March. People on the base are calling me 'General' already, but it's a little embarrassing right now."

Perhaps that's why he was taking orders instead of giving them last week. He was back in West Manchester where his parents—Leo and Desneiges Lamy—are engaged in a major home improvement project and Perry was happily playing Indian to his father's chief.

In fact, he was hauling insulation around the house over on Varney Street when I caught up with him, and yeesh, did we have some catching up to do.

Little things, mostly.

You know, like him graduating from the U.S. Air Force Academy—he was tops in his class in thermodynamics and propulsion—and flight training school and those two master's degrees and that internship at the Pentagon and his hitch with the United Nations Command in South Korea which should not be confused with the time he spent with the Strategic Air Command and hey, let's not overlook his own career as a big-time, hot-shot experimental test pilot, since he personally commanded the test crew on Ronald Reagan's baby, the B-2 Bomber.

"It's every test pilot's dream," he said, "to be a part of a new plane. I worked on the B1-B, too. I picked up Airplane No. 28 from the Rockwell factory in Palmdale and it was kind of like picking up a new car at the dealership. With a car, you make sure the radio works and the defroster works. With a plane, it's radar and flight controls and weapons bays."

Test pilots call it "pushing the envelope," this chance to work with new and experimental aircraft, but it was another kind of envelope—one containing a telegram—that helped him get where he is today.

"It's funny how a day like that stands out in your mind," he said of a certain spring day in 1971. "My dad was a foreman over at Bee Bee Shoe and he got jobs for me and a bunch of my friends from West, so I'd walk across the bridge after school and work from three o'clock till seven. He got out at 4:30 so he'd come back and pick me up. I thought it was strange that day because my brother was in the car with him but we got home and my mom met us at the door—all smiles—and on the table, there was the telegram."

The telegram was from U.S. Sen. Norris Cotton.

Perry had been accepted to the U.S. Air Force Academy and when he was graduated in 1975, his dream—the dream that started when he was in the first grade—was coming to fruition.

"I was one of those '60s space nuts," he confessed. I remember staying home from school the day Alan Shepard went up. A Derry guy? I thought that was really neat. The Mercury 7 guys were all my heroes."

He proved it in the seventh grade at Sacred Heart School.

"We had to do some kind of class play about what you wanted to do for work," he said—and this will get him a lot of grief if it gets back to the base—"so I dressed up like a pilot. I wore my dad's old Army Air Corps hat and a pair of headphones from the basement.

"I had done some research, and back then, I knew if you wanted to be an astronaut, you had to be a test pilot, and if you wanted to be a test pilot, what better place than the Air Force? Once I got into high school, that's when I started thinking about going to a military academy."

It's not like he wasn't accustomed to wearing a uniform. He was a Star Scout in Ray Bellemore's legendary Troop 135 at the Sacred Heart parish, but all the merit badges in the world can't compare to getting a set of wings pinned to your chest.

He got his in February of 1977.

Since then, he's flown B-52s and F-111s and T-38s and 30 other types of aircraft. He's logged more than 3,700 hours of flying time— think of it as an hour a day, every day for more than 10 years—and that's not counting the year he spent flying a desk at the Pentagon.

"There are only like 70 captains a year who get picked for that internship," he said. "They do it to expose you to the budget process and see how decisions are made."

It must have worked.

He made the decision to marry the former Peggy Solomon when he got that assignment and after 17 years, two sons and 15 different postings, she is still—to mix a military metaphor—his anchor. You need one when you choose a life in the service of your country, but for all of his devotion to duty, Perry hasn't forgotten the life he left behind.

"I have this little plastic model of a boot from Prevue Products," he said. "My father gave it to me before I left home. He said, 'I've worked all my life in a shoe factory. Here's a reminder of where you came from. When times get tough, look at this and think about the opportunity you have.'

"It was his way of telling me to work hard and get an education. For the last 30 years, I've had that boot with me. It was on a shelf in my room at the Academy and if I had an office it was in my office and if I had a desk, it was on my desk."

He's back at his desk in California now and his mom—like most moms—has mixed feelings about it. "We always knew he'd do something wonderful in his life," said Mrs. Lamy. "We just wish he was closer to home, that's all."

Maybe he will be.

He's only 46. Should he decide to retire, he could always make his way back home and find work. In the meantime, he kind of likes it where he is.

"There is no question I can pump gas with the best of them," he laughed, "but I'm still at the 'it's-a-pleasure-to-serve' point. As long as I feel like I'm needed, as long as I feel that I can make a contribution and as long as I'm having fun, I'll stay with it. If I'm not having fun, it will be time to move on, but right here, right now?

"I've got the best job in the Air Force."

(8/14/00)

Operation: Recognition

IN THE 60 YEARS SINCE his classmates were graduated from Manchester High School West, Paul Boisvert has never attended a class reunion.

"I didn't graduate," he explained, "and I respect their territory."

Paul didn't graduate because he enlisted in the Army. While his classmates were studying English and history, he was in basic training. Later, he would go to England and help make history.

In time, he took part in the invasion of Normandy. He survived the carnage at St. Lo. He witnessed the "shooting gallery" at Falaise. He was there for the liberation of Paris, he fought off the Nazis and the cold at the Battle of the Bulge and ultimately he helped liberate an Allied POW camp in the mines at Nordhausen, Germany.

He's seen more history than today's students will ever read, but he never had a sheepskin to show for it. "That's OK," he said. "When people would ask, I'd say I went to the school of hard knocks."

That's not what it will say on his diploma.

Paul Boisvert will get his diploma—the West High diploma that eluded him for more than 60 years—today at 1 p.m. That's when he will join 25 other veterans of World War II and the Korean War on stage at the Memorial High School auditorium for a most unique graduation ceremony.

It's called Operation Recognition.

"And it's long overdue," said Cindy Driscoll, who is coordinating the event for the Manchester School District.

For the first time, a school district in New Hampshire will present high school diplomas to those whose commitment to country interrupted their formal education. All told, 31 diplomas will be issued— three posthumously; two in absentia—from both West and Central high schools, largely because a Korean War veteran named Stavros

Included among the 31 Queen City veterans who received high school diplomas during Operation Recognition were, from left, Ernie Battistelli, Edwin Babel, Jean Boutin and Paul Boisvert. (Union Leader Photo by Bob LaPree)

Stefanos Moungelis pressed the issue with school officials.

"It's been a void in my life, the one thing I did not complete," said the retired Marine Corps captain, "but from a non-selfish perspective, I view this as a golden opportunity to impress upon all concerned— teachers, parents, alumni and especially students—the value of a diploma and the importance of staying in school."

Stavros would have been graduated from Central High in 1952. Instead, during his 20 years in the Marine Corps—"20 years, six months and 13 days," he noted—his lessons came not in the Classical Building, but in Korea and later in Vietnam, where he took part in the 1968 Tet Offensive.

In this instance, the Maryland resident took the offensive once again and his persistence will be rewarded when he gets his diploma an hour after he steps off U.S. Airways flight 2698 from Baltimore.

"I learned my lessons from the guys who went off and fought World War II," he said. "It's good that they're being recognized."

The urgency attached to the event struck home Monday. That's when one of today's scheduled honorees, Roger G. Jacob—an Army veteran who was wounded at Anzio—passed away at the New Hampshire Veterans Home in Tilton.

"They say we're losing 1,100 of them every day," said Dennis Viola, director of the New Hampshire State Veterans Council. "Basically, by the year 2008, the World War II generation will have passed, so if we're going to do these things—recognize the sacrifice these people made—we need to do it now."

Roger Jacob will receive his diploma posthumously.

So will William Towne—the Army veteran, who served in both India and Burma, died in July—and Lawrence Martel, whose widow is working to make certain her children and grandchildren and succeeding generations know what her late husband went through at the Battle of Leyte Gulf.

"He was on the U.S.S. Samuel B. Roberts," Lorraine Martel said.

That destroyer escort, known affectionately as "the Sammy B," was sunk by Japanese naval bombardment on Oct. 25, 1944. Eighty-nine men died in the bombing and its immediate aftermath. For more than two days, survivors were left to fend off sharks, the elements and the enemy while praying for rescue.

In the end, 120 men were saved.

Lawrence Martel was among them.

"I was married to him for 48 years, and I never knew what he went through until the end," she said. "When they were in the water, a Japanese battleship passed by them at night. He said the Japanese sailors on the ship looked them right in the eye, but they never shot at them. They figured the sharks would get them."

When Lawrence Martel came home from the war, he married, raised two children and worked as a master weaver at Chem Fab. The three years he spent at Central High School before joining the Navy weren't enough for a diploma.

Until now.

"What they went through—especially at such a young age—they acquired a lot of knowledge fast," Lorraine said. "That's why this means a lot."

A lot of the graduates were reluctant to apply for Operation Recognition when Tom Brennan—a former assistant superintendent now working in New London—was taking the program through its early stages. In many cases, the veterans did so only at the insistence of family members. Candidates were asked to provide information about the schooling they were able to complete in Manchester, broad details of their military service and proof of honorable discharge.

They were also asked to provide a photograph of themselves in uniform. Not for means of verification, but to provide material for what may be the most remarkable high school yearbook ever assembled in Manchester. The photos show men—very young men—on ships, at airfields and standing before bullet-riddled walls.

Still, for all of the courage these men displayed in the battle against tyranny, there are butterflies aplenty regarding this brief venture into the public eye. In fact, many of these brave men would rather face enemy fire than set foot on stage today.

"Back in the '40s, we used to say praise the Lord and pass the ammunition," said Jean Boutin. "Well, I'm just praying to the Lord I don't have to speak. I don't want the spotlight on me."

Like Paul Boisvert, Jean Boutin would have been graduated from West High in 1940. Instead, he joined the Army. Ernie Battistelli would have been graduated from Central in 1943. Instead, he joined the Marine Corps and Carl Burnap would have been graduated from Central in 1945. Instead, he joined the Navy.

"I was on an LST, a Landing Ship Tank," he said. "On D-Day, we went into Gold Beach with the Canadians. We were right next to Omaha Beach. I don't know what I was doing with the Canadians, but that's where they put us."

Before he was through, Carl's ship made 50 crossings of the English Channel, he ferried tanks up the Seine River for the Battle of the Bulge and he served with the Allied Occupational Forces in Japan.

After he was discharged, he got his GED, then he got a bachelor's degree from Keene State College, then he taught industrial arts at Central High for 33 years. Clearly, he knows the value of education.

He knows the value of a diploma, too.

"Next Friday, my graduating class at Central—well, my so-called graduating class—is having a 55th reunion," he said. "They've always included me even though I wasn't in the yearbook, but this time, I can bring my diploma. Maybe after I have a drink or two, I'll even show it to them. I'm the newest member of the Class of '45."

Actually, he's in the Class of 2000.

There are 31 men in his class.

As a group, they will forever be in a class by themselves.

(11/4/00)

Pen Pals

THE FIRST TIME FRANK LUGO got a letter from Cassandra Perry, it was quite a study in contrast.

There he was, standing in the 120-degree heat of the Saudi Arabian desert, wearing the combat camouflage of the U.S. Marine Corps. At age 21, a burly leatherneck on his way to war in the Persian Gulf—his .50-caliber machine gun slung over one shoulder and bandoliers of cartridges criss-crossing his chest—bent to examine the delicate penmanship of an 11-year-old girl.

In that very moment, a letter from half a world away, addressed to "Any Service Member," helped forge a bond between a lance corporal and a six-grader—a bond that is very much alive today.

The bond was strengthened when Cassandra and her parents—Dennis and Theresa Perry of Manchester—rendered Lugo speechless by secretly flying to his home in Bakersfield, Calif., to join in his welcome-home party in 1991.

And it was reinforced Tuesday when Lugo returned the favor by flying across the continent to spend Christmas with the Perrys as a surprise to his young pen pal.

"My mother had put a little star on the calendar, but I had no idea what it meant," said Cassandra, now a 15-year-old sophomore at Manchester Memorial High School. "I should have known, though. I've been trying forever to get my father to put Christmas lights on the house, and this is the first year he did it."

No matter how much those lights shine, they won't brighten Lugo's day any more than the first letter he got from Cassandra.

"It was just a real nice letter," he said. "She didn't ask what kind of gun I used. She didn't ask if I had killed anybody. More than anything else, I needed to get away from that, and she just wrote about stuff at home.

They were worlds apart in every sense, but the war in the Persian Gulf helped forge an unusual bond between Cassandra Perry and Lance Corporal Frank Lugo. (Union Leader Photo by John Clayton)

"She wrote about her school (St. Anthony) and her cat (Lucky) and her hamster (the now-deceased Minnie), and I just had to write back."

"I think he wrote me maybe 30 times," Cassandra said, "but he had to stop just before they went into combat. We watched the news every night on TV, and I was scared."

"You wrote me way more than that," Lugo said yesterday, glancing at a stack of their correspondence on the Perrys' kitchen table.

Before they were through—Operation Desert Shield had become Operation Desert Storm and Operation Desert Storm had become an overwhelming allied victory—more than 130 letters had passed between them.

Four years later, a continent stands between them, but their friendship—a friendship forged by mail—has bridged that gulf.

It was in another gulf, the Persian Gulf, that Lugo learned so much about friendship.

"Maybe it's the fact that I was adopted as a child, but I guess there's a thing they call 'separation anxiety' or something, the fear of being left behind," he said. "I've always worried about that, and then when two of my friends from my unit were killed in the war, well, it just means a lot to me to stay close to people."

He's been close to the Perrys this week. Mrs. Perry planned to introduce him to students at Southside Junior High School, where she works as a teaching assistant, and Cassandra wanted to drag him to Memorial.

And then, although they may not be able to deliver on the white Christmas that Lugo wanted to see, they also have shopping, skating and sight-seeing trips planned, including visits to the Atlantic Ocean—Lugo has seen the Pacific and Indian oceans, but never the Atlantic—and to the White Mountains.

He hopes he'll be able to keep up.

In the years since the Gulf War ended, Lugo has been hospitalized for damage he suffered to both knees during a rocket attack. Because of those injuries, he was forced to leave the Marine Corps. Now, after three years of physical therapy, he has a clean bill of health and, provided he survives his holiday "vacation," he plans to enlist in the Army in March.

As a combat veteran, he hopes to be posted to Korea.

Where, no doubt, he's sure to find a letter waiting.

(12/23/94)

City workers like Roger Olheiser tend to the bronze plaques that occupy places of honor in streets and squares around Manchester, the better to remember those who gave their lives for their country. (Union Leader Photo by Bob LaPree)

Preserving Their Memory

THEY GAVE THEIR LIVES for their country, so we in Manchester honor them with bronze plaques in squares that bear their names. But even today, Memorial Day—when the tablets erected in their memory are bedecked with flags—these monuments can be easily overlooked.

If we aren't careful, the men they honor may also be forgotten, and the fallen sons of our city might be lost in the mists of history.

Does anyone know Granite Square as "Little Square"? Nearly 80 years ago, that was the name bestowed upon the busy West Side crossroads in honor of Army Pvt. Herman F. Little.

But who was Herman Little? He was just an average Joe, supporting his widowed mother by working as a wool sorter with Amoskeag Manufacturing. Then, in 1918, he enlisted, trading the tranquil streets of Manchester for the trenches of Europe. In no time, he found himself on a boatload of doughboys bound for a French village on the Western front.

Little was with the Sheridan Guards attached to the 103rd Infantry. Their task? Prevent the Germans from crossing the Marne and reaching Paris. They did it well. Then, on July 18, under the leadership of Marshall Foch, he took part in a ferocious counteroffensive that drove the Germans back into Belgium.

On Aug. 6, his mother received a tersely worded telegram from Washington.

"Deeply regret to inform you that . . . Private Herman F. Little, Infantry, was wounded in action July 20. Degree undetermined. Department has no further information."

That same day, Anna Little got a letter from her son dated July 3.

"We are having a hot time . . . with the Huns," wrote Little, who told of meeting another West Side boy—William Gemmell—in the trenches. "I gave him a little advice on how to battle the Huns, as he is new in the game and I am an old hand."

Not very old. In fact, Pvt. Little was already dead at the age of 22 when his mother read his letter. She wouldn't learn of his passing until Sept. 6, but he had died in the field at Chateau-Thierry on July 20, and a grateful city—moved by his valor—erected a plaque in his honor.

☆ ☆ ☆

Every day, hundreds of shoppers come and go at Sully's Superette on South Main Street, but in the rush of traffic, how many have time to notice the plaque across the street that honors the memory of Seaman Francis "Pat" Lally?

Even if they had the time, the plaque has only the barest of facts. Seaman Lally died with his shipmates when the escort carrier Liscombe Bay was torpedoed off the Gilbert Islands on Nov. 24, 1943.

It says nothing of his days at West High or at St. Anselm College or about his part-time job at Sully's. Nor does it record the selflessness that earned him headlines a year before his death.

While off the coast of Guadalcanal, his ship came upon the carnage that was once an American destroyer. Three days earlier, a squadron of Japanese planes—32 in all—had sunk the ship and returned three times to strafe the survivors. The sharks took their share as well. One of the men they pulled from the water was another West Sider named Bob Phillips, who soon felt the hand of a friend.

"I could not walk or see as I was blind from oil in the water which had gotten into my eyes," Phillips later wrote in a letter to his mother. "As the ship pulled up, Pat says he recognized me. He carried me down to his bunk, gave me his clean clothes and took care of me until we got into port and to the hospital. He let me have his bunk and slept on the floor right beside me. He sure was a wonderful friend if there ever was one, and I'll never forget it."

Manchester hasn't forgotten Lally either. The Southwest Little League named its field in his honor, and a corner of the city still carries his name.

☆ ☆ ☆

When he left St. Joseph's High School after his sophomore year, there wasn't much doubt that Roger Cote was going to join the Army.

But enlisting at 17? He couldn't do that without his father's signature, but his was an Army family, after all, so William Cote gave it willingly.

Perhaps that's why the sight of two men in uniform at his door cut him so deeply. It was Sept. 11, 1950.

"We were all there when they brought him the telegram," said Private Cote's brother, Arnold Cote, who was just 12 at the time. "My father just walked out the door. He walked around for a long time. Then he came back in. He told us my brother was dead. We already knew."

Ten days earlier, Pfc. Roger B. Cote had been killed in action near Masan in South Korea. His death still haunts his cousin, Raymond Cote.

"I think of him often," he said. "We had a whole bunch of kids in the neighborhood. We'd vault over Cemetery Brook and hunt for pollywogs, all those Huckleberry Finn things kids did back then. I still wonder how things would be if he was around."

If you drive past the point where Valley and Massabesic streets converge, he is still around, at least in memory. That's where his mother and father and brothers and sisters gathered on June 17, 1951 as the city of Manchester named the square in his honor.

☆ ☆ ☆

Many other Manchester men have been honored with bronze plaques, but the facts engraved upon them convey too little about the men themselves. The same is true of those whose names live on in our parks and schools and bridges.

To better know them, Mike Lopez and Tony Karam from the Greater Manchester Veterans Council are compiling information for a book. They want stories and anecdotes and personal remembrances from friends and family so those who made the supreme sacrifice can be remembered by future generations.

"We need to know who these men were," Mike said. "We have some information, but we want more. We need newspaper clippings and photographs. We want to verify what we have and expand it so we can create a book and place it in every school in the city."

They need your help, because we need to remember.

(5/27/96)

Memorial Day seemed the perfect time for Tony Karam, left, and Mike Lopez to issue a booklet entitled "Manchester's Honored Veterans." (Union Leader Photo by Bob LaPree)

Manchester's Honored Veterans

THEY WERE SUPPOSED to be remembered. Now they will be. Since its founding, Manchester has named its parks and streets and squares and commons in honor of valiant veterans, but over time, as their faces have faded from our memories, their stories have faded as well.

How fitting then, on Memorial Day, that their stories should be resurrected. They are stories of courage and valor and sacrifice, stories of ordinary men thrust into extraordinary circumstances, stories contained in a new book called "Manchester's Honored Veterans."

The stories are like that of William Jutras.

☆ ☆ ☆

To many, the name Jutras is only associated with the American Legion Post that bears his name, but Lieutenant William Jutras gave more than his name to a legion hall. He gave his life for his country, and the quality of that life can be measured in the valor of the men who tried to save him.

In September of 1918, he was with the 103rd Infantry in St. Mihiel, France, when the American forces were divided by German troops. After volunteering to serve as liaison with those who had been cut off, Jutras delivered his message, only to be cut down by machine gun fire as he made his way back to his unit.

Jutras lay but 100 yards from a German machine gun nest. That's when Sgt. Cyrus Wallace and Cpl. Herve L'Hereux, a friend from Manchester, raced to his aid. As they tried to drag him to safety, they too were in peril.

"We could no longer keep low," L'Hereux wrote, "but had to stand right up and walk. As soon as the enemy saw us, they opened up on us . . . The Red Cross man had a band on his arm and we had no guns, but they shot at us just the same. They tried in vain to get us, but it was no use, as God was protecting us."

All but Lt. Jutras.

L'Hereux and Wallace carried him through barbed wire entanglements, a muddy swamp and a field still filled with artillery fire. They sheltered him with their own bodies so stones and earth would not fall on his face, "but we did not mind this," L'Hereux wrote, "for our only thought was to save our man."

They failed, but not for lack of valor.

Jutras died the next day, Sept. 26, 1918.

☆ ☆ ☆

Through the years, names like William Jutras and Rene Gagnon and Christos Kalivas and Ben Bronstein and Jean Grenier and Henry Sweeney have become part of the fabric of Manchester's landscape.

But why?

"That's what we wanted to show people," said Legionnaires Tony Karam and Mike Lopez. "We wanted to create a book to remind people who these men were and what they did."

So Karam started writing and Lopez petitioned the Greater Manchester Veterans Council for start-up funds to assemble a book. They gave him $500. As much as money, they also needed material. They turned to former Manchester Mayor John Mongan and this writer for research.

We found stories, stories like that of David Crossett.

☆ ☆ ☆

David Crossett never got to hear that famous song about Bette Davis' eyes, but it didn't matter. He found out about them first hand.

He was fresh out of Central High, working in the kitchen up at Peckett's in the White Mountains. He'd studied "culinary accruement" and it came in handy when a summer resident from Sugar Hill decided to order something that wasn't on the menu. She wanted a Waldorf salad, so Crossett whipped it up.

Moments later, he was beckoned to the dining room.

"This is Miss Bette Davis," the maitre d' said. "She wanted to thank you."

She gave him a $5 tip.

"It made David's day, of course," said his sister, Carolyn Harris. "He said she had the most beautiful blue eyes."

As blue as the Pacific Ocean, which Crossett crossed soon after. He'd enlisted in the Navy and drawn the most exotic duty he could imagine. His post: Pearl Harbor.

That's where he was on Dec. 7, 1941. When the alarms shattered the silence on that sleepy Sunday morning, he was aboard the USS Utah, so he scrambled to his duty station up in the crow's nest. A Japanese fighter strafed the ship. Crossett was shot twice. He fell to the deck. As further damage was inflicted on the Utah, his body was covered with debris. It was Dec. 16 before his family was notified of his death.

Manchester was hit hard in that first battle of the second World War. Maurice St. Germain, Joseph Rozmus and Joseph Jedrysik also died at Pearl Harbor. And for the Crossett family, their grief was compounded on June 30, 1945, when David's brother, Army Pfc. Carleton Crossett, was killed at Okinawa.

Crossett is typical of the men in "Manchester's Honored Veterans." While some, like Kazimieriz Pulaski and Marquis de Lafayette are of another time and place, the others are men from this city and of this city. They went to school at Bakersville and St. George's and the old Hevey Street School, just like us, and they worshipped at Sacred Heart and St. Patrick's Church, just like us.

Just like Henry Gossler.

☆ ☆ ☆

Henry Gossler was a West Sider through and through. He grew up at 151 Thornton St., and like so many of his neighbors, he even worked at the H.B. Reed shoe shop in McGregorville. However, the French he heard on the job was different than the French he heard when he was shipped to France in April of 1918.

By October, after he had endured eight months of battle, he heard encouraging news. In a letter, he told his family so, but figured the details wouldn't pass muster with the censor. They think he caught wind of the pending Armistice.

It didn't matter though. On November 1, 1918—just 10 days before the war would end—he was shot dead in the Argonne Forest.

When his body was returned home, his family was able to identify him by the contents of his pockets. They found a picture of his sister and a prayer she had sent him. The prayer was stained with his blood.

Gossler Park School was dedicated in his honor on Jan. 20, 1957.

☆ ☆ ☆

Thanks to the generosity of individual donors and sponsors, 1,000 copies of "Manchester's Honored Veterans" have been printed. Ed Girard and Paul Nelson at Lafayette Press defied all deadline odds to complete it for Memorial Day.

Except for the printing costs, all of the work was donated, even the Bob Dix cover illustration, but a token charge of a dollar per book will help offset the cost of printing and allow free copies to be distributed to schools throughout Manchester. Copies can be obtained by contacting Sweeney Post at 623-9145.

"From the beginning, our goal was to give the people of Manchester something to remind them of these men," Lopez said. And Karam added, "Memorial Day seemed like the right time."

(5/26/97)

The Tiger Cruise

THE PERSONNEL MANIFEST for the USS Theodore Roosevelt will be undergoing a few changes before the Nimitz-class aircraft carrier steams into Norfolk Naval Base in Virginia next Thursday.

The revised roster goes something like this:

- Ship's Company: 3,200.
- Air Wing: 2,480.
- Marine Detachment: 35.
- Grandmothers: 1.

At the risk of venturing into Aldrich Ames territory and divulging highly classified information, we shall identify the grandmother in question as Paulette (Gagne) Vincent, a 57-year-old mortgage originator from Hooksett who will be making her maiden naval voyage this weekend.

Her mission: A reunion with her son, AZCS Marc Vincent, 37, who serves as chief of the flight deck on one of the largest warships in the world.

Paulette's presence on board comes thanks to a unique U.S. Navy program called "Tiger Cruises," a progressive public relations venture that will bring as many as 500 other civilians to the carrier for the final four-day leg of its six-month deployment.

According to U.S. Navy spokesman Lt. Brian Kelly, it's a way to give friends and family—no spouses, for reasons that should be obvious—a chance see what life is like aboard ship, and to experience the emotion and excitement that accompanies "homecoming," as sailors and Marines are reunited with other loved ones after a long mission.

And getting on this trip has been a mission for Paulette.

"Marc's father and grandfather got to go aboard the USS America with him when they came back from the Persian Gulf," she said, "but

Paulette Vincent found a bully pulpit aboard the USS Theodore Roosevelt when the Hooksett mom joined her son on the aircraft carrier for a family-oriented Tiger Cruise. (Union Leader Photo by Bob LaPree)

back then, they didn't have accommodations for women. I always felt like I'd missed out on something special. Ever since then, I've been bugging Marc to see if he could get me on board."

As senior chief on the "TR," Marc Vincent doesn't take orders from a lot of people, but—let's be honest—mothers outrank everybody, so he convinced a female shipmate to co-sponsor his mother's visit.

"I couldn't stay in the men's section of the ship," she explained, "so now I have a berth in the women's quarters."

She had to lay out her fair share of quarters to make the trip in the first place, because this is no taxpayer-financed junket. "Tigers," as they are called, must pay for their flight to Norfolk and for a subsequent charter flight to Bermuda. They'll spend Sunday night there—they pay their own hotel bill, too—before being ferried out to the "TR" where, once again, they'll pay for their own meals and incidentals.

"But we eat in the regular mess right alongside the sailors," Paulette said. "That's a big part of the experience, seeing what their lives are like on board, and I think the chance to live like Marc does will be great.

"It's something he loves dearly—he's been in for 18 years—and I think it's great that he'll have me there. I don't know how many men would be that excited to have their mothers on board their ship."

Of course, it isn't like she's a landlubber. In their travels around the country, the Vincent family has had boats on Lake Erie and on the Mississippi River, and just three years ago Paulette sailed on a windjammer off the coast of Venezuela.

"We got caught in a horrible wind storm," she said, "and I spent the whole night out on the deck. It was just an experience I didn't want to miss."

She felt the same way about the Tiger Cruise, especially after listening to her father, retired deputy fire chief Ovila Gagne of Manchester.

"I expected to have a lot of restrictions on the ship but there were none," he said. "They showed us everything from the engine room to the missile launchers. We watched the take-offs and landings on the flight deck. They couldn't have treated us better. The whole experience was spectacular."

Her father's enthusiasm has proved infectious for Paulette, although she is intrigued by the reaction her adventure is drawing from friends.

"All the men say 'Geez, you must be excited,'" she laughed, "but the women all ask things like 'Aren't you afraid you'll get seasick?'"

Based on her vocabulary, it seems unlikely. The naval terminology that spills from her mouth makes her sound like an old salt, although the "old" part seems to fit her not at all.

"When my father went, he was 77, and the captain told him he was the oldest man on board," she said. "Some of the officers might be older than me, but even if I'm not the oldest, I know I'll be the only grandmother on board."

(5/16/97)

Meeting The Enemy

 THE MOMENT OF TRUTH for Ed McKenzie—the moment that would shape and color so much of his life—came on April 24, 1944.

He was folded into the ball turret gunner's position, a delicate glass pocket in the belly of a B-17 Flying Fortress. The bomber, dubbed the Toonerville Trolley, was in formation, making its way back to its home base in England after raining its payload down upon the Dornier Aircraft Works near Munich.

Air Force records say the mission was a success.

"The attack by the 92nd and 384th bomber groups of the 41st Wing climaxed about 1400 hours," according to the official report, "and was considered by the German high command to be the heaviest against the Dornier works to date, possibly because of its high precision."

From his precarious perch—certainly the most vulnerable position in the aircraft—Ed McKenzie was able to witness that precision. He had little time to savor the success, however.

"Here they come!" barked a voice over the tiny intercom. "Fighters! Twelve o'clock. Right at us!"

The fighters were German Focke Wulf 190s. They were small, fast and maneuverable—everything the lumbering B-17s were not—and the Luftwaffe pilots, Hans Berger among them, now had the Allied formation in their sights.

With his guns blazing, Ed McKenzie tried to track the swift German fighter planes, but his efforts were cut short.

"Something slammed into my ball turret," he said. "I must have seen it coming, since my hands went up in front of my face. My fingers were numb and my gloves were torn. There was a blast of wind hitting me. Some objects went streaking past me, and one of them was a huge three-bladed propeller, certainly from a B-17."

Plaistow native Ed McKenzie, who now resides in North Conway, was aboard a bomber dubbed the Toonerville Trolley when it was shot down over Germany. (Photo by Lorna Colquhoun)

It could have been a propeller from his B-17, the Toonerville Trolley, and life for Plaistow native Ed McKenzie—just two months past his 19th birthday—was about to change forever.

☆ ☆ ☆

It was a lovely spring day in the Bavarian village of Bubach. It was planting season in the lush Oster Valley, a peaceful time, until the flaming American bomber screamed from the sky above.

There was a tearing, crunching sound.

Then all was still.

"And the shock of reality hit me," Ed recalled. "I was alive, but on the ground deep in the heart of Nazi Germany and would not be going back to my base—nor to my home in New Hampshire—probably ever again."

Not that he wasn't going to try.

Even as the dust inside the aircraft began to settle, Ed and two remaining crewmates—others had bailed out before the crash—began to scramble for cover. Top gunner Ed Kolber, who had been wounded in the fire fight, had no choice but to stay with the plane and surrender.

"I was lucky I got out of the ball turret before the crash," Ed said. "It's a good thing I did because the belly of the plane was flush with the ground. The ball turret was disintegrated, so when the plane finally had come to rest, we went blindly out of the top hatch, slid off the wing and headed into the woods."

The flight on the ground, much like their flight in the air, was short-lived.

"From all directions," Ed recalled, "people came carrying hoes, rakes and pitchforks, all wanting to help apprehend the enemy soldiers. A local leader of the farmers carried an old rifle with him and waved it in the air to emphasize his direction in apprehending the flyers."

That civilian band succeeded in capturing Ed and his remaining crewmates. All were unarmed, as ordered—"If we were lucky enough to be on the ground and alive, we weren't expected to carry on a hopeless shooting war as individuals," he said—and their civilian captors marched them off to a stone barn.

Pilot Bill Hamilton feared they were headed for a firing squad. He wasn't off by much. They were headed to a POW camp in Austria.

It was Stalag 17.

☆ ☆ ☆

Those memories—now more than 50 years old—are still fresh in Ed McKenzie's mind, perhaps because he has committed them to paper. He did so in a fascinating reminiscence called "Boys at War, Men at Peace," but on that day in April of 1944, he knew that peace, at least for him, was a long way off.

"We had more than 4,000 men in that camp," he said, "sharing each other's lice and what little food there was. I guess we were near starvation most of the time. One time two men tried to cut through the fence, but the guards spotted them and started shooting. The first fellow they shot to death and then they hit the second man."

That second man was Ralph Lavoie of Rindge.

After Lavoie was hit, the guards stopped firing, but an officer walked up, stood over the fallen flyer and emptied his pistol into him. As the officer was reloading, the Allies' camp leader, Kenneth Kurtenbach, went out to protect him. The prisoners looking on figured both POWs were dead, but Lavoie survived. He was shot six times, but he survived.

Forget about the movies. That was life in Stalag 17.

"It was my home for just a year," Ed said. "The last month of the war, we were on the road. We were marching to stay ahead of the Russians. Neither the Germans nor the Americans wanted to get caught up with the Russians. They considered their own soldiers to be dead once they were captured, and we heard they felt the same way about American prisoners. The ones they found, they ended up in the gulag."

Fortunately, as they neared the Inn River on the German-Austrian border, the POWs and their Nazi captors encountered American troops first.

"One of Patton's armored divisions was on the other side of the river," Ed said, "and we got someone over there under a white flag to let him know we were Americans. We got there just in time, too, because they were just about to start shelling us.

"They sent an American captain over in a Jeep with a driver and he got up on the hood of that Jeep and he told us we were free," Ed said. "People described him afterwards and they said he was all of 8-feet tall, a big handsome captain, and you know what? In their eyes, he was all of those things."

☆ ☆ ☆

When Ed got back to the United States, he was processed through the Veterans Administration Hospital in Manchester. He had to sit for a "protocol" physical and, like all former POWs, he also underwent a psychological exam.

More than 50 years later, his crewmates probably wondered whether Ed passed that last test. In 1996, German historians and civic leaders in the area where the Toonerville Trolley went down—led by researcher Klaus Zimmer—tried to organize a reunion of those who were involved in the downing of the American bomber.

"In that area," Ed explained, "the biggest thing that ever happened to them was this plane coming down. It became an important part of their history."

For most men—historical significance notwithstanding—the initial wartime experience would have been enough to last a lifetime. Any reminder, however slight, would be too much to endure. But three years ago, Ed McKenzie made history come alive when he traveled to Bubach and came face-to-face with Hans Berger, the Luftwaffe pilot who shot down his plane.

"Just the chance to meet with the townspeople who remembered the crash was almost enough to make up my mind to go," he said, "but then when I got word they had found the Luftwaffe pilot, well, that just made it that much more exciting.

"I wondered for quite a while what I would say to him and how I would react," he admitted, "but I found out he was going through the same thing. He said it first. He said 'This is much more pleasant than our previous meeting isn't it?' I agreed.

"Hans shot down three B-17s during the war, and he was happy to learn that on at least one of them, that everyone had survived," Ed said. "There were tears in his eyes to meet someone after 52 years who could bear witness to that fact.

"And you know," he added, "I was just as pleased to hear that he had survived. We had to destroy their air force so they couldn't support their troops. There weren't that many German fighter pilots who made it."

Today being Veterans Day, there are many who will speak to the topics of war and remembrance. And Ed McKenzie, who will ride today in the Veterans Day Parade in North Conway, is living proof that there is something to be said for forgiveness as well.

(11/11/99)

While his landmark series on the Civil War rekindled interest in the War Between the States, the 11-hour epic also established Ken Burns of Walpole as the leading documentary filmmaker in America. (Associated Press Photo)

"The Civil War"

 "ANY UNDERSTANDING of this nation has to be based on an understanding of the Civil War. It defined us. It was the crossroads of our being, and it was a hell of a crossroads."

—Historian Shelby Foote

More than 125 years after the firing ceased between Union and Confederate soldiers, the United States is still feeling the effects of the war.

It was a battle fought over the greatest moral issue in our nation's brief history—slavery—and the racial strife spawned by that issue continues to this day.

It was a war that pitted brother against brother, father against son, a war that—regardless of the technological advances of modern warfare—claimed more American lives than any war before or since.

Yet still, there exists a sanitized notion of the war.

"As a subject, the Civil War has been smothered for 125 years in gallant, bloodless myth," said filmmaker Ken Burns, who resides in Walpole. "People tend to romanticize and idealize both the Northern and Southern approaches, but in fact, this was indeed a time of our near national suicide."

Through his production company, Florentine Films, and with financial underwriting from the General Motors Corp., Burns took five years to chronicle the Civil War—longer than it took to fight the war itself.

Educators, critics and historians alike have praised the film, which brings the Civil War to life through the use of rare archival footage, thousands of historical photos, period paintings and music, newspaper headlines and first-person quotes from the era read by a chorus of distinguished voices.

"It is a cultural treasure," historian Bernard A. Weisberger said.

"Ken Burns makes it possible to understand at the deepest level how the hearts of that generation were touched with fire in a battle of ideas fought with passion and pain by flesh-and-blood people."

It is the flesh-and-blood element that is most tangible in "The Civil War," for not only does Burns focus on prominent figures such as Abraham Lincoln, Frederick Douglass, Robert E. Lee and Jefferson Davis, he also brings the war to light through the eyes of slaves, nurses and the rank-and-file foot soldiers he refers to as "spearcarriers."

"We follow the lives of two soldiers in the film, Elisha Hunt Rhodes of the Second Rhode Island, and Sam Watkins, a Southerner from Company H, First Tennessee Regiment, because these soldiers helped to give the war its meaning and sense of really having happened," Burns said.

"Still, we're most proud of the way that we've been able to correct 125 years of outright lies about the role of blacks. We had been taught that they had been passive bystanders to their own deliverance, when in fact, they were the most active factor, forcing upon Union commanders and President Lincoln the necessity of issuing the Emancipation Proclamation, and then by taking a most dramatic and heroic role in fighting for their own liberation."

There are also liberating aspects to the script of "The Civil War"— liberating in that screenwriters Burns, Geoffrey C. Ward and Ric Burns avoid the cautious, circumspect phrasing that characterizes so much history.

Instead, we get colorful descriptions that bring the characters to life, such as Stonewall Jackson—"a pious, blue-eyed killer"—and Gen. Benjamin Butler, "a man with crossed eyes and mixed motives."

The writers are also willing to let the events of the war carry the narrative whenever possible, and to let viewers absorb the war's uncanny coincidences in a gradual fashion. How uncanny? Consider the prospect of Robert E. Lee—the eventual commander of the Confederate army—leading federal troops to stop abolitionist John Brown at Harper's Ferry. Or, at Brown's hanging, the presence of a soldier in the Richmond Greys named John Wilkes Booth.

Such coincidences abound in Burns' film, coincidences that would defy belief in a conventional Hollywood film.

"There's not a Hollywood studio head who could invent the stories the Civil War has to tell," Burns said. "The little town of Winchester, Va., changed hands 72 times. A Confederate major bombarded a

Union flotilla in Texas, only to board the Union boat and find his son, a federal lieutenant, on deck, dying.

"Over and over again, the authentic record is more compelling than anything our imaginations could come up with," he said. "All we had to do was listen to it and arrange it in a way that would bring back a generation lost in the great pageantry of this war."

The pageantry of the war is artfully recaptured by Burns on film, and dramatically rendered by the voice of David McCullough, who served as narrator on several of Burns' earlier films.

Still, it is not the war's pageantry that stays with the viewer when the last credits of Burns' film fade from the screen. It is the cause of the war that stays with the viewer—slavery.

Thomas Jefferson likened slavery to holding a wolf by the ears. "You didn't like it, but you didn't dare let it go," historian Shelby Foote said, in quoting Jefferson. In raw numbers, one out of every seven people in America was owned by someone else when the Civil War began, but just as people have forgotten the numbers, so too have they forgotten the moral legacy of slavery, according to Burns.

"For 125 years, we've masked over the reason for fighting this war, which was the stain of slavery," he said. "It is a stain that even today we are struggling to erase. In some ways, the Civil War is a moral parable for the way we are today.

"We're still trying to understand how a nation could be founded on the premise that all men are created equal and yet enslave millions of its own. 'The Civil War'—this documentary—is an attempt to wake us up to our own birthright, to gain knowledge of who we are, but the main thrust here is the story, the great compelling narrative of the Civil War. There's no better American story."

And no better American storyteller.

(9/16/90)

Captain Bill Eagleson was no stranger to the B-24 Liberator, nor was he unfamiliar with the local terrain when he landed at the airstrip once known as Grenier Field. (Union Leader Photo by John Clayton)

The Liberator

 LIKE THOUSANDS of other servicemen, Air Force Maj. Carl Gikowski, a B-24 pilot, passed through Grenier Field in Manchester during World War II. From all accounts, his stay—a fog-bound, eight-day stretch—was not a pleasant one.

Here's his diary entry from Oct. 9, 1944:

"The field is the most miserable I have ever been on," he wrote. "Since we are a transient crew, enroute overseas, we are restricted to the field. We are very anxious to leave. . ."

Too bad he didn't serve with Capt. Bill Eagleson.

"If he was with my unit, he'd have been over the fence on the first night," he grinned. "Then he'd have had the chance to meet the people. They were so good to us. That's what made Manchester so special."

That's what made Eagleson's return so special.

After more than half a century, he soared—no, he roared—back into the Queen City on Tuesday afternoon, this time as part of a vintage aerial convoy that included a B-17 Flying Fortress and the last flying B-24 in the world.

"A lot of lumps in my throat," he confessed, as he gazed about the civilian aviation complex now known as Manchester Airport. Eagleson was only 24 when he first set eyes on the field. It was early in the winter of 1944, just after he earned the last of the 30 silver bombs emblazoned on his flight jacket.

He was a bombardier aboard a B-24, a member of the 453rd Bomber Group attached to the 8th Air Force. From their base in Old Bucknam, England, Eagleson's unit conducted bombing runs in support of the D-Day invasion. They also delivered the goods over Nazi Germany.

"We flew missions over Berlin, Hamburg, Hanover, Munich," he said. "Our only night mission was over the Ruhr Valley. We were on our way to Hamm. I'll never forget it. We dropped our bombs at dusk, so we were silhouetted against the sky. The German planes could see us from below, but we couldn't see them."

The journey back was eventful.

"There was technicolor flak and German night fighters and RAF night fighters and we had to make our landing with no lights on the field," he said. "They'd all been shot out."

It's understandable, therefore, that his post-combat stay in Manchester—while placid—remains so vivid.

"After combat flight, being reassigned to Grenier Field was like going to the office," he said. "In at 8:00, out at 5:00. John L. Moore was the commanding officer—we used to call him 'The Silver Fox'—and Arthur Maynard was the civilian who ran the officers club.

"We used to hang out at The Elms. They had a little ski hill over there, and we took our troops over and taught them how to ski by the rope tow," added Eagleson, who was assigned to run the base's athletic program.

"We used to pull our basketball players from all over the northeast," he said with a grin. "The 'Grenier Field Skyhawks.' We were good. We played at Boston Garden. We played against UNH and Springfield and Middlebury and every time we played on the base, the people from Manchester would come out and fill the gym. They were so good to us.

"That plane was good to me too," he said, with a nod toward the gigantic B-24 Liberator that's been dubbed the "All American."

Such planes were a familiar sight over Manchester throughout the war years, which makes the Liberator's visit all the more poignant. This is the last of its kind. More than 18,000 were produced during the war, and this is the only air-worthy craft that remains, so it is an emotional symbol for the men who served aboard similar airships.

"We had to deal with bitter cold, sometimes 50-below," Eagleson said. "We had a 10-man crew, and you had to watch out for things like anoxia, freezing oxygen masks . . . but it always got us home."

Today, Eagleson makes his home in Natick, Mass., but he'll be in Manchester tomorrow. He's part of a team from the Collings Foundation that has restored the aircraft so veterans and civilians alike can travel back to a different era when the skies above Manchester were darkened—and yet, somehow brightened—by the presence of the B-24.

(9/26/96)

The President's Own

 YOU'VE HEARD THE EXPRESSION "banned in Boston"? Well, this is about a band in Washington. Or perhaps I should say *the* band in Washington.

It's called "The President's Own" United States Marine Band, and given the general parameters of this book, you have probably deduced that there's a man in the band from New Hampshire.

His name is Jason Fettig.

Make that Staff Sergeant Jason Fettig, a 1993 graduate of Central High School who now belongs to—and I'm not going to mince words here—the finest band in the world.

Now, I know there are folks around here who think Jason could have made that same claim when he was at Central, but rather than start an interscholastic war waged with glockenspiels and flugelhorns, let us put our partisan positions on hold and learn a little bit about this national treasure known as "The President's Own."

It was 1798 when President John Adams brought the band to life. For starters, that makes it the oldest professional musical organization in America. In the intervening two centuries, the band has played at every Presidential inauguration. It's rumored the band even got Calvin Coolidge to tap his toe. (But I doubt it).

"The President's Own" accompanied Abraham Lincoln to Gettysburg, they were there when they laid the cornerstone for the Washington Monument, they played at Grover Cleveland's White House wedding and at the request of the first lady, they led the procession for the funeral of John F. Kennedy.

In short, the band is as much a part of American history as the guns and butter debate—its music was among the first to be recorded by Thomas Edison—and now a young man from Manchester is a part of it all.

There's no mistaking the uniform of The President's Own United States Marine Band, nor is there any mistaking the musical gifts of Manchester's Jason Fettig. (Photo Courtesy of Mr. and Mrs. William Fettig)

"For us, this is the equivalent of having somebody make it to the NBA," said David Bresnahan, the Central High School music director who helped nurture Jason's skills early on. "It's a fabulous honor for Jay, but it's also a tremendous thing for our students to use as a benchmark. For me, it can be a great motivational tool."

Jason's "tool" with the United States Marine Band is the clarinet. Specifically, it's a B-flat clarinet. He's one of 25 clarinetists in the band, and if you think he got the job because the uniform fit, think again. Earlier this year, 35 euphonium players auditioned for a single position.

No one made the cut.

Only the best need apply.

"I believe he was auditioning with 200 other folks for his position," Dave said. "Almost all of them have experience with symphony orchestras, many of them have doctorates from music schools"—(Jason has a BA from UMass)—"and he beat them out."

Perhaps it's that kind of exacting standard that prompted The Washington Post to print the following eye-popping statement: "The U.S. Marine Band demonstrated once again that it is not only the best in the land, but very likely, the world."

A bold claim? Almost as bold as the brilliant scarlet uniforms that serve as the band's standard performing attire. That's what they're wearing—all 148 of them—at today's performance at the Hubble Middle School in Wheaton, Ill.

Hey, you can't play Carnegie Hall every day.

"It's a 50-day tour," Jason said. "We did almost all of our rehearsing before we left, so once we're on the road, we play every night. We'll be in Ohio, Illinois, North and South Dakota, Minnesota. Pretty much all over the place."

When he's not on the road, Jason makes his home in Alexandria, Va., But even when he's home—since the band plays about 200 times a year at the White House—he spends a lot of his time at the home of the President.

"The first time I went there, we went in a side gate and boom, I was standing 10 feet from the White House looking up at the south portico," he said. "I was pretty awestruck. I'm like everybody else, so I'd always seen it from 200 yards away, behind the fence with the other tourists."

He's not a tourist anymore, and what with the regular performances for visiting kings and queens and potentates, he's probably met his share of royalty, right?

"Actually," he laughed, "at my first White House gig, I got to pet Buddy the dog."

Jason never did say if Buddy was much of an audience. Even if he was, though, it would be tough to top the audience at George Mason University where 250 kids from Central High's band and chorus got to see him play.

"That was a great thrill for the kids to see one of their own playing with 'The President's Own,'" Dave said. "After the concert, he came out and talked with the kids and it was just fabulous."

Equally fabulous was the music, which has always been Jason's strong suit. He began playing the clarinet when he was in the second grade. He also knows his way around the drums and the piano and—like one-time band leader John Philip Sousa—he's not exactly uncomfortable with a conductor's baton in his hand.

"The reason he was chosen to be drum major at Central was because he had such musical mastery," Dave said. "I could have been absent during band camp his senior year and no one would have known I was missing."

It doesn't hurt that Jason comes from a musical family. His mom and dad, Bill and Kathleen Fettig both have vocal backgrounds and his brother Adam, a senior at Central, also plays the clarinet and sings with the chorus.

Good genes only go so far, however. Then talent and hard work take over.

"My parents did urge me to start early," he said. "Most kids start clarinet in the fifth grade, not the second, but from the beginning, it was very natural for me. As I got better though, it got more and more difficult to make steps to the next level."

There is no "next level" for him any more.

A spot in this band—"The President's Own"—is as good as it gets.

(10/26/98)

An Unknown Soldier

CERTAINLY THEY NEVER met. The two men lived in different worlds. But Chris Karaberis was the kind of man F. Scott Fitzgerald had in mind when he said, "Show me a hero and I will write you a tragedy."

It was on Nov. 11, 1945 that Manchester and all of New Hampshire turned out to honor Sgt. Christos H. Karaberis. He was the grand marshal of the Armistice Day parade, riding in a limousine down Elm Street.

Thousands of spectators ignored the steady drizzle and pressed forward as the open car crept down the wide thoroughfare, for the object of their attention was affixed to a ribbon around the neck of the small soldier. It was a reminder of the "conspicuous gallantry" with which he served in Italy.

It was the Medal of Honor.

Today, half a world away, Christine (Karaberis) Huston dreams of that medal. To us, it represents nothing less than our nation's highest military honor. To her, it stands for even more. It represents a piece of her legacy, a part of her family history. It's a seminal link to a father she never knew.

It's a medal she would cherish.

If only she could find it.

☆ ☆ ☆

In the close-knit Greek community that crowded together in Manchester during the early years of the Depression, young Christos Karaberis seemed to fit in easily. Classmates at Hallsville School speak of a hard-working but quiet boy whose education ended before high school.

He had little say in the matter. His family needed money so he left

President Harry Truman presented the Congressional Medal of Honor to U.S. Army Sgt. Christos Karaberis at the White House on Oct. 12, 1945. (New Hampshire State House Photo)

school early to work with his father at a shoe shop in Ipswich, Mass. That's where he met Elinor Sotos.

Unbeknownst to friends and relatives in Manchester, Chris started a family with Elinor. They had three children together. The births—and the paternity—are a matter of public record. There are no such records of a wedding, so the issue of marriage is subject to speculation.

There is no speculating about war, however, and so it was that Chris entered the U.S. Army at the outset of World War II. He was shipped to Italy. He served in L Company, 337th Infantry, with the Fightin' 85th—the Custer Division—when he found himself staked to an unforgiving hillside outside Guignola. His squad's objective was the Casoni di Remagna, another fortified village on the endless road to Rome. It was Oct. 12, 1944.

They had been making their way through a small ravine when his platoon was pinned down by a barrage of mortar shells and machine gun fire from above. In the half light of dawn, Chris set out alone to silence the enemy guns.

As he scaled the hill, he ignored the gunfire that ricocheted around him. He moved up and to the left, the better to circle behind the emplacements. The dim light served him well, as he startled the occupants of the first machine gun nest with a burst from his own weapon. He took eight German prisoners, returned them to his unit and set out again.

This time there was no element of surprise.

"Discovered in his advance and subjected to direct fire…he leaped to his feet and ran forward, weaving and crouching, pouring automatic fire into the emplacement that killed four of its defenders and forced the surrender of a lone survivor," according to his Medal of Honor citation.

Next, with an ear-piercing scream and a burst of gunfire, he charged yet a third machine gun emplacement head-on. In the face of his maniacal attack, four more German soldiers threw their weapons down and surrendered.

Operating solely on adrenaline, he pressed ahead again, this time toward two more German batteries. His first burst of fire took out four Germans. Three others surrendered and, in the words of his citation, "the six defenders of the adjacent position, cowed by the savagery of his assault, immediately gave up."

The reward? In a theater where progress was measured in inches he helped his unit claim five hundred yards of Italian dirt. Better yet? No casualties. Not in Italy anyway.

☆ ☆ ☆

While Chris Karaberis was battling the enemy in Europe, his three children were engaged in a struggle on the home front. The stakes were equally high.

Friends in Manchester who have vague memories of the situation say their mother, Elinor Sotos, was unable to care for them. Welfare officials said the children were being neglected. Against the protests of their grandfather—Athos Karaberis—they were taken away.

"We were put into an orphanage in Boston—The Home For Little Wanderers," Christine said. "From there, we lived in a series of foster homes. When I was 4, my brother and I were together, then my sister was with us for a short time, but then we were dispersed into different homes.

"When we were small, we were told our parents were killed in a car accident. We never questioned it. It wasn't until we were grown up that we began to ask questions."

The answers to those questions were troubling. Did their parents marry? No one knows. What became of their mother? No one knows. And Christos Karaberis, this decorated war hero, did he search for his children when he returned? No one knows that either, and that's what troubles Christine the most.

"I'm trying to understand it all," she said. "I hope that maybe my father was trying to find us all those years, but I don't know. The people I've contacted in the Greek community in Manchester have been wonderful to me, but there are so many things they don't know. What I do know is that he's gone, and I have so few links to my past."

☆ ☆ ☆

Christos Karaberis had largely escaped from his own past when he died on Sept. 16, 1970, out in Huntington Beach, Calif. He had a new wife, new children. He even had a new name. Out there, he was known as Chris Carr. The name enraged his parents, who were fiercely proud of their Greek heritage.

Christine Karaberis Huston shares that pride, even though she never knew her grandparents, just as she never knew her father.

Today, at 59, she lives with her husband in Saudi Arabia. She has five kids of her own. As fate would have it, one of them—Paula

Durost—lives in Weare, so there are reasons for her to visit the area and seek out old family ties that are new for her. She treasures visits with her father's cousins, John and Jim Barakis, just as she still treasures her father's memory.

"I have a picture of him wearing it, but I want to know what happened to his Medal of Honor," Christine said. "Did he donate it to a museum? Was he buried with it? I've contacted the military, and I've tried to reach the children he had in California, but so far, I haven't found any answers.

"I'd love to have the medals he won and frame them with his photo," she added. "I want my kids to know they had a grandfather who was a hero, who risked life and limb for his country."

(11/10/95)

The perils of military service struck home when friends and relatives gathered to bury Wade Elliot Hector of Newport, who was killed in a truck accident while serving in Saudi Arabia. (Union Leader Photo by John Clayton /Inset by Associated Press)

...With the Thanks of a Grateful Nation

Faded yellow ribbons were everywhere yesterday, as the funeral cortege of Wade Elliott Hector wound its way south along Route 120 to Mill Cemetery in Meriden.

They were affixed to car antennas, mailboxes and fence posts as the line of cars stretched out over the 12-mile ribbon of roadway from the West Lebanon Baptist Church to the windswept hill near the Connecticut River Valley that will be Hector's final resting place.

The ribbons that came to symbolize hopes for the safe return of American troops represented a hollow irony for the mourners who gathered in memory of Hector, the 22-year-old National Guardsman from Newport who died in a truck accident in Saudi Arabia on Feb. 21, 1991.

Perhaps that is why spirits began to soar as the procession moved past East Plainfield into Meriden, where American flags snapped in the breeze, brilliant in the late-winter sunshine.

At the crest of a hill, where dozens of flags flew outside Kimball Union Academy, students and staff members lined the roadway, many with hands over their hearts, in salute to Hector.

"I could just hear Wade saying, 'Wow, all this for me,'" said his aunt, Phyllis Leavitt. "He was such an unassuming young man. He would be overwhelmed."

It was with full military honors that Hector was laid to rest yesterday, which seems only fitting for a young man whose passionate patriotism compelled him to enlist in the National Guard immediately upon his discharge from the Army.

But the young soldier who lost his life during Operation Desert Storm was more than a military man, as friends and family paused yesterday to remember a young man whose enthusiasm for hunting, hiking and camping was boundless.

His mother, Freda Washburn, recalled how his letters from Saudi Arabia would always open with the salutation "Howdy," in stark contrast with his starched military bearing, while his fiancee, Gayle Dennis, spoke of the fanciful drawings that would illustrate his letters.

The gray clapboard church was filled to capacity as the Rev. Dean Eggert delivered the eulogy alongside Chaplain (Lt. Col.) Richard Thompson of the New Hampshire Army National Guard and his Air Force compatriot, Chaplain (Col.) Charles Crosby.

Among the mourners were Gov. Judd Gregg, U.S. Rep. Richard Swett and Maj. Gen. Lloyd M. Price, adjutant general of the New Hampshire National Guard.

Immediately upon graduation from Lebanon High School in 1986, Hector enlisted with the United States Army and served three years in Germany. And once again, immediately upon his discharge, Hector enlisted in the New Hampshire National Guard, and it was with colleagues from the 744th Transportation Co. of Claremont that he was shipped to the Persian Gulf on Jan. 10.

The accident that claimed his life also claimed the life of Todd Christopher Ritch, 20, of Claremont.

During graveside services at the Mill Cemetery yesterday, five soldiers fired three volleys in salute to Hector, and after a lone bugler sounded taps, National Guard representatives presented American flags to Hector's mother, his fiancee, and his father, Eugene P. Hector of White River Junction, Vt.

Also present at graveside were 40 somber cadets from nearby Norwich University, classmates of Hector's younger brother Blaine.

The gray-uniformed cadets formed an honor guard in tribute to Hector, but it was a tribute of a different sort, from students of another school, that provided the day's most moving spectacle.

(3/2/91)

The Merci Box Car

THEY'VE BEEN DOING THIS for nearly 50 years now, but as usual, there were curious looks and puzzled glances as the dignified men of *Le Grande Voiture 40 & 8* paraded down Bremer Street on Manchester's West Side yesterday.

Their destination?

The Merci Box Car.

Tucked away on a short, dead-end stretch of Reed Street, this extraordinary—some would say unusual—token of affection from the people of France is an often overlooked piece of history. Overlooked, that is, by all but the members of the 40 & 8, the veterans fraternal organization whose members long ago vowed to preserve the rail car, and its significance, for future generations.

And so they convened again yesterday, as they do on the second Sunday of every October, to remember their fallen comrades—"the Voyageurs"—who have passed away since last they gathered here.

The procession was a grand one, some 150 strong. The pageantry was provided by the American Legion Band from Keene's Gordon Bissell Post and the women's auxiliary and a host of uniformed color guards from throughout New Hampshire, all of whom gathered outside the brick and glass pavilion that houses the box car.

But what is it about this old gray railroad car, now empty, that fills it with such significance? Why have men like Fred Teague and the late Donald Still invested so much time and energy toward its preservation?

To know that, one must go back to 1947, a time when the people of America came to the aid of France. Not as military allies, this time, but as friends of the embattled French people.

Even two years after the end of World War II, food and clothing were in short supply throughout much of Europe, so the American

Frederick Teague and his fellow members of Le Grande Voiture 40 & 8 have kept their promise to preserve the Merci Box Car in West Manchester. (Union Leader Photo by Bob LaPree)

people, with prodding from newspaper columnist Drew Pearson, responded by sending a 700-car "Friendship Train," laden with relief supplies, to the people of France.

In return, the people of France responded with a symbolic train of their own, a "Thank You Train"—hence the *Merci* Box Car. As the train traveled though the towns and villages and provinces of France, citizens were encouraged to fill the tiny cars with personal mementos and artwork and photographs and letters and other tokens of gratitude for the people of America.

The response? More than 250 tons of "gratitude" filled the train by the time it reached port at Le Havre, and an additional 9,000 gifts had to be left behind when the French cargo ship Magellan departed for New York Harbor.

When it docked on Feb. 3, 1949, the ship carried 49 box cars, one for each of the 48 states and one to be shared by the District of Columbia and the territory of Hawaii.

The odd-looking cars were not unfamiliar to American servicemen. Long before they became links in a gift to America, the 40 & 8 boxcars had a special place—for better or worse—in the hearts of American fighting men.

During World War I, most khaki-clad doughboys bound for France reached their American port of departure on roomy Pullman sleeper cars. Once in France, however, their journey to the front lines frequently came in the tiny 40 & 8 boxcars.

The origin of the name? It's simple enough. It's based upon the capacity of the box car itself. In transporting men and materiel to battle, the cars were capable of carrying 40 men or eight horses.

In French, that's *"Quarante Hommes et Huit Chevaux."*

Understandably, the Yanks were either amused or repulsed by their means of transit, and then there was the sergeant who, as they say, got lost in the translation. "I got all my 40 artillery-men in the box car," he told his lieutenant, "but if you try to put eight of our horses in, somebody's gonna be trampled to death."

Experiences like that—for better or worse—formed the basis, in 1920, for the good-natured formation of the 40 & 8, the "fun" American Legion subsidiary known formally as *"La Societe des Quarante Hommes et Huit Chevaux."*

And, some 29 years down the line, who better to take responsibility for the box car than the organization that took it as its *raison d'être?* In

New Hampshire, it made perfect sense, and for those of us who care about such things, there could not have been a better choice.

As proof, consider the unfortunate outcome in other states where the Merci Box Cars have been subjected to varying indignities down through the years.

In Idaho, for instance, the historic box car is situated at the Idaho Penitentiary in Boise, hardly a reminder of international friendship. In Nebraska, the gift from the French people was sold for scrap. Sale price? Forty-five bucks. In other states—like Connecticut, Rhode Island and New Jersey—the cars were destroyed by fire.

In still other states, the cars are dying from benign neglect, something the Grand Voiture of New Hampshire vowed would never happen here.

"I didn't get to see it the day it arrived in New Hampshire, but I remember when it got here," said Teague, 71, a Navy veteran and retired carpenter who serves as volunteer caretaker for the box car and the pavilion in which it sits.

It's a responsibility he takes to heart.

"I feel it's part of the heritage of this country," he said, "and someone has to keep it up. I know a lot of people have forgotten why it came here in the first place, and I just wish we could make it so more people knew what it stood for."

It's hard to tell how many folks remember the day the box car first arrived in Manchester. It was Feb. 10, 1949. Thousands gathered at Elm and Market streets outside City Hall to see the car, adorned as it was—and still is—with the colorful coats-of-arms of the 20 French provinces.

Its treasures, in accordance with the wishes of the French people, have since been scattered amongst the schools and libraries and veterans organizations of the state. All that remains in the box car itself is a single bronze vase, a gift from one Monsieur Lavertu from *"le Bibliotheque, Ville de Cherbourg."*

The greatest treasure? That's still the box car itself. That, and the members of *Le Grande Voiture* 40 & 8 who, true to their word, have kept it for all to see.

(10/13/97)

The Last Boy in Blue

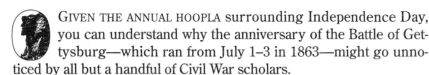GIVEN THE ANNUAL HOOPLA surrounding Independence Day, you can understand why the anniversary of the Battle of Gettysburg—which ran from July 1–3 in 1863—might go unnoticed by all but a handful of Civil War scholars.

And maybe, just maybe, by those who remember James Marion Lurvey.

Lurvey was the last survivor of Gettysburg. He was there as a drummer boy attached to the Union Army of the Potomac and when he died in 1950 at the age of 102, he had outlived every one of New Hampshire's 33,937 Civil War veterans. He's buried in Londonderry, just down the road from the home in the Manchester area of Goffe's Falls where he spent the last 60 years of his life.

The most important year of that life, however, was 1863.

The events of that year—more specifically, James Lurvey's role in those events—have consumed Jay S. Hoar, a professor of English at the University of Maine at Farmington. He has invested 40 years of research into the Civil War service of New Hampshire's "Last Boy in Blue."

"It's ruled my life," Hoar said of Lurvey's story. "I was 16 years old when I met him. It was 1949. I'd never been away from home, but when I saw his picture in *Life* magazine, I knew I had to meet him."

Hoar hitched a ride from his Maine home to Plymouth, New Hampshire, then hopped a train to Manchester. After a night in the Floyd Hotel—"It was three dollars a night," he said—he took a city bus to Lurvey's home at 2915 Brown Ave.

Hoar's visit is a story unto itself, but the story Lurvey told Hoar qualifies as pure Americana.

James Lurvey was just 14 years old when he enlisted in the Union Army. His mother allowed it simply because he was going to serve

141

James Marion Lurvey was the last survivor of the Battle of Gettysburg, but there was another battle—a battle with the law—still awaiting the Union Army drummer boy. (Photo Courtesy of Cora Lurvey Smith and Professor Jay S. Hoar)

with his father, Lt. James T. Lurvey, then 36, who was commander of Company A of the 40th Massachusetts.

"I remember Grampa once told me that when people asked why he wanted to join the fighting, he said 'For the Negroes,'" his granddaughter recalled. "Then he went on to explain that he had never seen a Negro."

The frail boy hadn't seen much at all, really. Certainly nothing that could prepare him for the horrors he was to witness.

Hoar's research found both father and son at Dumfries, Virginia, in December of 1862, when Confederate Gen. J.E.B. Stuart tried to disrupt Union supply lines. While his father went on to further battle at the Siege of Suffolk in April and May of 1863, young James—weak and sickly—went on to Campbell Hospital in Washington.

"It was mainly so he could gain strength and return to duty," Hoar said.

When young James was released from the so-called "Invalid Corps," he was ordered north to Pennsylvania, where, in Hoar's words, "the Confederate invasion promised an impending battle of unknown magnitude."

At Gettysburg, that battle was joined on July 1. Young James did not arrive until the next day.

"But July 3 and very probably July 4—could he have eliminated any two days of the 37,554 that he lived—surely they would have been these," Hoar said.

Lurvey's recollections:

"I never fired a shot," he said. "At Gettysburg, I was still a drummer boy (but) during much of that battle I served in the Medical Corps. Shot and shell and the screams of dying men and boys filled the humid air. A non-com told me to put away my drum. He tied a red rag around my left arm and told me I was now in the Medical Corps.

"I told him I was not big enough to lift my end of a stretcher, so he assigned me to a field tent," Lurvey added. "It was stifling inside. I thought I'd keel over when they told me my assignment. Wish then I could have hefted a stretcher.

"I was to stand by and carry out the soldiers' arms and legs as the doctor amputated them," he said. "I guess that was the day I grew up and left boyhood forever. And I wasn't yet sixteen."

His daughter, Cora (Lurvey) Smith, died in Londonderry 10 years ago at the age of 100, but she, too, was fascinated by her father's stories of Gettysburg.

"I recall his saying that one hot day, he crawled into a pup tent in the shade and went to sleep. Soon after, someone pulled him out by the feet and told him a soldier had just died of smallpox in that tent. Luckily, he didn't contract it.

"He said many times when crossing a river or pond, some big strong soldier would take him across on his back," she said. "Many times water to drink was scarce, and after a rain, the men were glad to drink from pools made by cavalry hoofs."

It's hard to gauge the after-effects of such psychological trauma on a boy, but three months later, young James was discharged at Portsmouth. The documents state: "By reason of youth—age 15—not robust."

"During the next 10 months," Hoar said, "he recuperated, added stature and strength and decided to try and improve on what he may have felt was an unimpressive military record."

To do so, he re-enlisted. It was during this second tour of duty, while at Monson Hill Camp near Falls Church, Virginia, that he first set eyes on the man whose integrity had called him to duty.

"He used to visit us in camp," young James said of President Abraham Lincoln. "He was no great sight—tall and awkward—but he had a great mind. He used to talk with us for the sake of cheering us up, I think."

Two months after Robert E. Lee's surrender at Appomattox, Lurvey was discharged from the Union Army. After working in the mica mines and traveling the world on a merchant marine clipper ship, he fell in love with school teacher Sarah McConnell of Haverhill, N.H. They married in 1874.

Raising four daughters in Goffe's Falls should have provided his remaining years with all the excitement he needed, but the legend of James M. Lurvey was not yet complete. In 1902, that legend took on even more mythical proportions when, at the age of 55, he was accused of robbing an American Express payroll—Butch Cassidy-like—from the Goffe's Falls train station that was bound for the local Devonshire Mill.

Although he constantly proclaimed his innocence, he was convicted. The jury asked for leniency—citing his war record—but he was sentenced to serve six to ten years in prison. When he was released, he seemed none the worse for the wear. He even managed to attend the 50th anniversary gathering at Gettysburg in 1913.

To this day, neighborhood children like Esther (Dancause) Theodore remember him well.

"We all knew who he was, that he had been in the Civil War," she said. "I can still remember walking to school in the morning. He'd be sitting on the porch and he'd always wave to us."

He did that until well past his one hundredth birthday. He told friends one of his proudest possessions was the congratulatory letter he had received from President Harry S Truman on that special occasion.

And as to the cause of his longevity? Well, Lurvey always attributed that to his sturdy ancestors and his "fortified" breakfast, a daily dose of coffee spiked with a shot of brandy he called his morning "oh be joyful."

That formula worked until June of 1949. That's when, two months after his wife passed away his daughter, Gladys Lurvey, reluctantly moved him into the Bedford (Mass.) Veterans Hospital.

"Gettysburg was tough," he told Hoar, "but old age is even worse. I'm older now than I ever wished to be. Nobody realizes old age is a hard life till they get there."

That hard life ended on Sept. 17, 1950, but thanks to Hoar, the legend of New Hampshire's "Last Boy in Blue" still lives on.

(7/3/98)

Gerry Grimard's name does not appear on The Moving Wall, nor does it appear on the Vietnam Veterans Memorial in Washington, D.C., but the circumstances of his death make him a victim of that conflict. (Union Leader Photo by Bob LaPree)

Agent of Death

OFFICIALLY, WHEN Gerry Grimard died Oct. 21, 1986, the cause of death was listed as cancer. Marjorie Grimard, the widow of the 39-year-old Vietnam veteran, thinks another cause should be listed—Agent Orange. Mrs. Grimard thinks the circumstances surrounding her husband's death—a swift but painful death attributed to liver cancer—sound too much like the circumstances surrounding the deaths of other Vietnam veterans. There was her husband's history of frequent headaches, the sudden appearance of skin lesions known as chloracne and ultimately, the diagnosis of the soft cell cancer that took his life. Mrs. Grimard, the mother of a four-year-old son, wants some answers.

Before Gerry Grimard donned the uniform of the United States Army in 1969, he was recognized most often in the blue and white football uniform of Manchester High School West. Grimard was an undersized fullback and linebacker who was renowned for the ferocity that earned him a spot on the Division II All-State football team and in the 1966 New Hampshire-Vermont Shrine Game. True to his aggressive form, Grimard missed his chance to play in the Maple Sugar Bowl when he sustained a concussion in his team's final drill. He spent the remainder of his visit to Hanover in the Mary Hitchcock Hospital. Ironically, 20 years later he would return there to await his death.

The steaming jungles of Long Binh in Vietnam are worlds away from the quiet, French-Canadian rhythms of Manchester's West Side, but it is a journey made willingly by Gerry Grimard in June of 1969.

After being graduated from the New Hampshire Voc-Tech in Manchester, Grimard enlisted in the Army knowing full well he would be shipped to Vietnam. His duties with the Army Signal Corps placed him firmly in the line of fire. Grimard, accompanied by emergency medical teams, would race to the site of downed American aircraft. While the medics sought out the injured pilots and crew members, Grimard would strip the aircraft of its radio equipment to keep the hardware out of enemy hands. As activity increased to the north, Grimard was moved to Quang Tri in the DMZ. While that transfer exposed him to more Viet Cong activity, it also increased his exposure to a more insidious killer—the chemical defoliant Agent Orange.

"He never talked about it," said Marjorie. "We were engaged when he was over there, and when he wrote, it was never about what he did. Once he got back, if people asked him about it, he just changed the subject.

"I tried to get, him to talk about it when he was sick, and that's really the first time he mentioned Agent Orange to me," she said. On the job, however, Grimard would occasionally raise the subject with co-workers.

"He was kind of a private person, but he had a concern about the spraying of the Agent Orange," said Dennis Lunderville, director of the State Division of Air Resources where Grimard worked for 14 years. "He knew his assignments had brought him out in the field where the spraying took place, but that was about the depth of what he would discuss. He never spoke negatively about his capacity with the military, but as time went on, he realized that the things that were being discovered after the fact placed him right in the middle of that whole mess."

In 1977, when Grimard underwent a routine physical, doctors detected an abnormal liver function. Since there was no history of liver disorder in his family, Grimard submitted himself to annual physicals until 1983, when doctors assured him his good health made it a needless exercise. In the fall of 1985, the discomfort began. It started with boil-like skin eruptions on his right hip. Although the condition cleared up in 10 weeks, the area remained scarred. By the summer of 1986, there were the sharp, intermittent pains in his right side, and by August, there was the fever. Doctors tested Grimard for a gall bladder infection, but results were negative. On Aug. 31, the day the Grimard's moved into their new home in Bow, Marjorie had to take her husband to the emergency room at Concord Hospital.

"They had to admit him because he had a high fever and chills, and they called for a liver specialist," said Marjorie. "The next day, they did a CAT scan and they found a tumor in his lower intestine. Then they found 'shadows' on his liver."

Surgeons removed the intestinal tumor, but Grimard's condition deteriorated rapidly. Plans to begin intensive chemotherapy in Boston for his liver condition had to be scrapped due to excessive blood clotting, so Grimard was transferred to Hanover instead. Ten days later, he died.

Since Grimard's death, a quiet pattern has emerged in the lives of Marjorie Grimard and four-year-old Kevin. During the day, she has her work as a paralegal in Concord, while Kevin has school to pass the time. The nights, however, are filled with memories. Some of the memories make Marjorie uneasy, like the memory of her husband's well-defined muscles wasting away in his final weeks, and the memory of one of her last conversations with him.

"The last week he was alive, the doctors said his cancer wasn't typical of a healthy man in his 30s," she said. "They told me it was typical of someone in his late 60s or 70s, and they couldn't understand how he could have so much cancer in him. I talked to him about finding out what caused his cancer, and when I told him I was planning to look into Agent Orange, he kind of laughed and said 'Good luck.'"

With the aid of U.S. Sen. Gordon Humphrey, Marjorie Grimard is trying to secure her husband's military medical records. On Tuesday, she received a large package of information from the Commissioner of Veterans Services of the Commonwealth of Massachusetts. It is just the latest step in a long process of acquiring information about the chemical defoliant that many believe has become the most painful legacy of America's involvement in Vietnam.

"It's going to take me a while, but I'm going to go through it all," she said, gesturing toward the pile of newspaper clippings, magazine reprints, medical studies and government pamphlets. In the meantime, Marjorie is finalizing plans for a $1,000 scholarship in her husband's name for a football player at West High.

☆ ☆ ☆

"After Gerry was graduated from West, we went to a game a few years later, and there was an older couple sitting in front of us," she said. "After a while, the man turned to the woman and said, 'West hasn't been the same since Grimard graduated.' Gerry just looked at me and smiled."

That pleasant memory brings a slight smile to Marjorie Grimard's face, but all too quickly, the glow is gone.

"Kevin was very close to his father, and it's just hard to know what effect this is all going to have on him," she said, "and I guess I feel that something happened to Gerry that shouldn't have happened. Even though the government and the chemical companies aren't admitting anything, Gerry went over there risking his life for his country, and they dumped all those chemicals on him that probably killed him 14 years later? I just think a lot of these things need to be brought out."

(1/22/87)

A Tribute Set in Stone

THE TREK NORTH from Berlin will begin about 10 o'clock this morning, but the original mission? The original mission began on July 11, 1944.

That was the day a U.S. Army Air Corps B-17 bomber left Kearney, Nebraska, bound for England by way of Bangor, Maine. As it moved from west to east, its flight path brought it over New Hampshire. Radio operator Cecil Murphy—one of 10 men aboard—made radio contact with Grenier Field in Manchester at 10:55 a.m.

That was the last anyone heard from B-17G 43-38023.

Military investigators out of Grenier Field think more than two hours passed before the Flying Fortress came out of the haze and the mist and slammed into a ridge near the top of Deer Mountain in the remote Maine wilderness.

There were no survivors.

"Can you picture that?" Mike Rozek of Berlin asked softly. "An 18-ton bomber slamming into the side of the mountain at 200 miles an hour? The largest piece they found was a three-and-a-half foot section of wing."

Even so, the unforgiving terrain surrendered little to salvage teams. In time, the military ordered in a bulldozer. After the live ammunition was removed from the site, the salvation effort was abandoned. The shards of the once-mammoth fuselage were simply plowed under.

Nature quickly reclaimed the site. For more than half a century, there has been nothing to consecrate the ground where those 10 men perished. Today, in a brief ceremony in the deep woods 10 miles from the New Hampshire border, Mike Rozek and a small contingent from the North Country will make amends for that oversight.

"I heard about the crash years ago from an old logger," Mike said.

Tiny pieces of wreckage are all that remain of the B-17 that crashed across the border in Maine in 1944, but North Country activists Mike Rozek, left, and Dick Pinette, made a monumental effort to remember the men who were lost. (Photo by Lorna Colquhoun)

"I figured if nobody else was going to do anything, then I would."

And he did. As a result, when the men from Berlin and Gorham and Errol gather today near the hamlet of Wilson's Mills in the unincorporated Maine township of Cupsuptic, they will do so around a 600-pound granite monument. It's a monument to honor those 10 servicemen. It's also a testament. A testament to Mike Rozek.

"It was all Mike's doing," said Richard Pinette, the North Country historian who pens the "Errol Echoes" column in the Berlin Reporter. "I'm just the water boy who set up the dedication. He made it happen."

What happened on July 11, 1944, has haunted Mike for years. He's only 44, but as a World War II history buff, he's always been struck by the way that war finds ways to touch our lives, even today.

"I had my own business on Main Street in Gorham for 18 years," he said, "so I got to meet a lot of people. One day I was having a conversation with a man named Ed Lemieux. He used to do some logging up that way and he told me about this plane that had crashed on the mountain. He didn't know what type of plane it was or exactly when it happened, but other people verified it and I wanted to know more."

His curiosity led him to his old auto shop teacher.

"Mr. Pinette had written about it in one of his books," Mike said— (the book is entitled "Northwoods Heritage")—"but all he had was what little bits he'd heard over the years. It really wasn't much, just that a B-17 bomber had crashed and been covered over by bulldozers, but it was enough to get me thinking."

He thought about it for years. He got a lot of anecdotal evidence, but nothing concrete. He pored through veterans magazines seeking information about the flight and the men on board. He also used the Internet for more digging, but in 1995, he caught a break. Thousands and thousands of military documents were declassified.

"They were all confidential records," he said, "but they would only release the information if it was a non-combat fatality. If this plane had been shot down in Europe, this information would not have been available, but I got it."

What he got was the official report filed on July 22, 1944 by Air Corps Maj. G.H. Shafer. It makes for gruesome reading, even in the clinical jargon of the military.

"The plane had evidently exploded with great violence," Maj. Shafer noted, "tearing it completely apart and scattering fragments over a wide area. All occupants had undoubtedly been killed instantly."

In graphic detail, Maj. Shafer recounted efforts to recover the bodies of the crew members. While the body of the co-pilot, Lt. John W. Drake, was formally identified, other remains were hard to come by. The circumstances became obvious to Mike Rozek a few years ago when he spoke to a neighbor.

"There's a man named Don Glover up in the area around Wilson's Mills," he said. "He told me one day a cousin of one of the men who died went to the site. As far as he was concerned, that's where his cousin is buried and he was devastated that there was nothing to mark it.

"To me," Mike added, "it was just a real sad state of affairs. I know that life goes on and everyone's too busy to stop. Well, I stopped."

His first stop was Nicoletti Memorials in Berlin. Mike asked owner Donald Piper about creating a permanent monument at the crash site. Don quickly offered up a 600-pound granite slab. No charge.

"I had no idea about the history or the tragedy until Mike brought it to light for me," Don said. "He felt strongly there should be something there to identify what happened at that location and I agreed. The only reason I got interested was because of his enthusiasm."

That enthusiasm quickly spread.

At Dick Pinette's request, the owners of the land—the Mead Corporation—gave written permission for the monument to be installed. Lucien Dupuis, commander of VFW Post 2520 in Berlin, volunteered an honor guard for the ceremony and Lionel Roy agreed to sing at the dedication.

Dick also took the time to write to Secretary of Defense William Cohen seeking financial support for the initiative. When the request was denied—"The department is unable to respond favorably to your request," wrote a Cohen underling—members of the Berlin-Gorham Rotary Club rose to the challenge.

Funds from the club helped defray the cost of engraving the names of the 10 servicemen into the monument, along with the following legend: "This W.W. II Memorial is dedicated to the crew of B-17G 43-38023 which crashed here on July 11, 1944. They gave their lives for their country."

And so it is that at 2 o'clock this afternoon, prayers will be uttered and men will sing and the colors will fly and 10 men—to the minds of those in attendance—will finally be laid to rest.

Mike, Rozek wasn't going to rest until it happened.

(7/15/00)

P.O.W.

IF THERE'S ONE THING that stands out for George Dargie on Veterans Day, it is the dress uniforms. Neat, crisp, clean. Sharp creases, starched and pressed just so.

He remembers when his own military attire was less spit and polish.

It was in 1944. He was in German-occupied Austria, heading for the Swiss border. He had escaped from a train filled with POWs. It was mistakenly bombed by Allied planes as it moved through the Brenner Pass, bound for Germany from Italy.

Weeks had passed since that escape, weeks spent underground with Chetnik rebels, but now Dargie was alone, eight kilometers from the Swiss border.

Less than five miles between him and freedom.

Then came the German patrol.

"They knew I was an escapee," he said. "I still had parts of my uniform on."

Once again, George Dargie was a prisoner of war.

☆ ☆ ☆

The merest hints of George Dargie's story are contained in "A Directory of New Hampshire Ex-POWs." It was compiled by Dr. F. Douglas Bowles and his wife, Madeleine Bowles, residents of Mirror Lake. The book contains information on more than 300 former POWs who call New Hampshire home, men like Bowles and George Dargie, who still lives in Manchester.

☆ ☆ ☆

"We were part of the assault force at Anzio," said Dargie, then a corporal with the 3rd Division of the Army's 30th Infantry. "On the

Prisoners of War like George Dargie don't need medals to remember their searing wartime experiences. (Union Leader Photo by Bob LaPree)

third day in, my company was overrun by tanks at the Mussolini Canal. Only two of us were captured. The rest of the company was wiped out."

Dargie suffered a stomach wound from a grenade. Medical treatment?

"We all carried sulfur powder in our packs then. That's all I had."

His wounds were ignored when he was bundled on the train to Germany. They were ignored after his recapture and at the POW camp in Moosburg, 25 miles outside Dachau. So he escaped again.

"The accommodations were lousy, you might say."

Again he headed for Switzerland. On the German shore of the Bodensee—the Lake of Constance—he found a homemade boat.,

"I had a piece of board for a paddle and I guess I made it halfway across when a German patrol boat came along," he said. "They had everything on board pointed at me. They got me again."

Not the next time.

"I decided to give up on the Swiss border," he said, "and headed into Poland."

In time, he crossed the Russian lines.

"I met up with a tank unit and walked up to them yelling the only Russian word I knew—'Amerikanski'—but they thought I was a German deserter. No one spoke English. I was on my way to Siberia, but an American intelligence officer, an OSS guy came in. I never let him out of my sight. When he went to the latrine, I went to the latrine.

"Two days later a C-47 came in with an officer who spoke perfect Russian. He told me to get on the plane with the other guy. The whole Russian Army couldn't have kept me off that plane."

☆ ☆ ☆

In the Bowles' book, Dargie's memories are listed tersely.
"Beatings. Hunger."
Patrick Reardon of Lincoln offered no memories.
But he remembers.

☆ ☆ ☆

The skies were quiet over the English Channel when "Southern Comfort," an American B-24, made its way toward Bremen, Germany, for a bombing run on Nov. 13, 1942. It was less quiet when the crew made its way back.

"We got hit with anti-aircraft fire and we went down over Holland. That's all we knew at the time," said Reardon, a gunner on board the aircraft who parachuted to safety with another crew member. Or so he thought.

"It took us a while to figure out we were on an island," he said. "We finally found a bridge and we watched it for a while. We saw people going across and we decided we'd try it. When we got halfway across, there were Germans on both sides. They had their guns leveled at us and we were unarmed, so we surrendered."

Like a lot of other American fliers—like Doug Bowles—Reardon wound up in Stalag XVII-B in Krems, Austria.

"Occasionally, you'd get some extra food from the men who went off on work details, maybe parts for the radio," he said. "I was a Red Sox fan, and when we were lucky, we could pick up the BBC. They might give a score, but sometimes any little memory of home like that would touch something off inside and you couldn't help thinking about getting back here to Lincoln, New Hampshire."

It was a year and a half before that day came.

"Part of Patton's army freed us," he said. "We'd been moved to

Braunau and they overran where we were in the woods. They didn't know we were there, so they weren't prepared to feed or clothe us. All they could do was protect us."

It was too late for protection from the guards.

"Some of the older ones acted like they could be decent," Reardon said, "but some of the others were grade-A bastards."

☆ ☆ ☆

In compiling the POW records, Bowles found that as bad as conditions were in Europe, servicemen in the Pacific Theater of Operations suffered more at the hands of their Japanese captors.

Japan was not a signatory at the Geneva Convention governing the treatment of POWs, and the Japanese "Bushido Code"—an ancient samurai tradition—meant POWs were subject to savage mistreatment.

Arthur Reynolds already knew that. So did Ralph Cullinan.

☆ ☆ ☆

In April 1942, Cullinan was in the Philippines with the Army Air Corps. Reynolds was too, but in a different unit. Unbeknownst to them, they would soon be linked forever in one of the war's most horrifying events.

The Bataan Death March.

For 98 days, Allied forces defended the tiny Bataan Peninsula against Japanese forces. In the end, they were overwhelmed by more than 200,000 Japanese troops. All told, 75,000 American and Filipinos were captured.

The forced march northward began immediately.

"They tried to put us in groups of maybe 500, and we set out, one group after another," said Reynolds, a Kingston native. "We had no food and no water. There were artesian wells all the way along, but if you went to them, you'd get shot."

If the jungle heat was brutal, so were the guards.

"Let's just say I've never heard a story I couldn't believe," said Cullinan, a Nashua resident who was beaten with a shovel when a wrenching bout of intestinal flu drove him into the woods. "I knew the odds of getting home were very bad."

The odds grew worse once they reached Camp O'Donnell, an abandoned Philippine base where thirst, hunger and disease claimed hundreds every day. That was their lot for three and a half years, and sometimes Cullinan and Reynolds wonder what it all means.

"People don't know about Bataan today," Reynolds said. "I went into a Marine recruiting office one time and there were a couple of young guys in there and they didn't even know what Bataan was. I guess people just forget after a while."

☆ ☆ ☆

Not if Doug Bowles has his way. His whole purpose in compiling the Directory of New Hampshire Ex-POWs was to prevent people from forgetting.

"I was just amazed that there wasn't a more complete listing some-where," said Bowles, a retired college history professor. "The more I inquired, the less I could find and then—maybe it was a weak moment—I said, 'I'll do it.'

"Once we started, it became even more important. The group is thinning out. The stories are being lost. We didn't want that to happen."

(11/11/97)

Paper carriers Frank Young, center, and Emile Bussiere, at right, were the bearers of glad tidings when America erupted in celebration on V-J Day. (Union Leader File Photo)

Victory

 NOT COUNTING NERO, the most superfluous musical performance in history took place 50 years ago today. Jess Stacey and his Famous Orchestra were playing at the Bedford Grove, but the boys in the band might just as well have left their instruments at home.

Who needed music?

In downtown Manchester, they were already dancing in the streets.

It was Aug. 14, 1945, and the war was over at last. After an anxious week of false alarms—a week in which hopes had been raised and dashed almost hourly—a radio flash at 7:03 p.m. caught the ear of an unknown soldier. He jumped from his table at the Puritan Restaurant and stepped onto Elm Street. His cry, according to newspaper accounts filed by Cpl. Norman Leighton, was simple: "The war is over!"

He should have been a headline writer.

The ensuing celebration was the most joyous in Manchester's history. Even though half a century has passed, those who were there will never forget the unplanned pageantry, the crying, the laughing, the tears and the cheers.

"I've never seen anything like it, before or since," said attorney Emile Bussiere, now 63, who was a 13-year-old hawking copies of The *Manchester Leader* alongside Frank Young in the midst of the maelstrom.

"One has to remember that back in those days, radio was the only means of electronic communication," he said, "yet there was no suggestion that people congregate on Elm Street. People just found their way there on their own, and what I will always remember is the feeling of euphoria."

Frank Young felt the euphoria. And claustrophobia.

"I was tiny then, and all I could see was ankles. I thought I was going to get crushed," said Frank, now 64, an attorney in White Plains, N.Y.

"Anytime there was a big event during the war, like D-Day or VE Day, I'd take all my money and buy as many papers as I could. Normally I'd run through the Millyard to sell them, but everyone was on Elm Street. The paper sold for a nickel a copy, but that night, I was getting a buck apiece from people. They were just so happy."

The newsboys were at the juncture of Hanover and Elm Streets— the hub of the hub-bub—along with thousands of others. It was a proverbial sea of humanity, and oceans of emotion spilled over. People felt an unspoken need to share the moment with others, people like Paula (Sandmann) Schulz, now 83, whose husband, Bill Schulz, was away in the Navy.

"Maybe it's because we were all so excited about our husbands coming home," she said, "but we just looked for friends and walked and talked with anyone we saw the whole length of Elm Street."

It was hard to be heard over the din. Air raid sirens wailed, church bells pealed and fire horns pierced the muggy summer night. At the Merrimack Common, kids clamored to clang the liberty bell at the Freedom House and car horns blared from "the Elm Street jalopy parade" that materialized as if by magic.

There was no time for ticker tape, so people improvised. From a third story window in the Week's Block, a young boy shredded newspapers and let the litter flutter to the ground. Others—mindful of the wartime paper shortage—made counterfeit confetti out of bread crumbs while still others filled the air with cursory concoctions of dry rice and beans. Popcorn was added to the mix when moviegoers began pouring out of The Rex, because no movie—not even Roy Rogers in "The Lights of Old Santa Fe"—could match the excitement outside.

The debris rained down upon the milling multitudes as Elm Street was quickly clogged. A horse and wagon laden with revelers clattered down the cobblestones after rolling all the way in from Pinardville and he growing ranks of celebrants were swelled even further by the arrival of night shift mill workers who'd been furloughed for the festivities.

First it was Holton Process, then Chicopee. Then Raylaine Worsted followed suit, as did Textron and MKM and Arms Textile and when the Waumbec workers left their looms and made their way out of the Stark Street gate, the uphill exodus was on in full.

"From then on," wrote Fred E. Beane, "it was one continuous howling, dancing, singing, yelling mass of humanity mixed up figuratively and literally with all the motor vehicles and bicycles in the city, about all the baby carriages, most of the babies, all of the good looking gals in town, soldiers and sailors by the hundreds, every kid in town."

Even a kid like Bob Cloutier, now 65.

"We were playing in the basement of Phil Gelinas' house at 356 Walnut St.," said Bob, "and as soon as we heard the news, we all went running down to Elm Street. We figured that's where the excitement was."

And how did Bob define excitement?

"Well, we figured we'd get kissed by all the girls," he laughed, "but we were only 15 so they pretty much ignored us."

But the girls? You couldn't ignore them. With their beaming smiles and their lipstick just so and their short sleeved summer dresses and the thin black line drawn up the back of their calves because there weren't any nylons in the entire country, even for special occasions like this.

Meanwhile, even as hundreds of youngsters were hanging on the idling cars, others were hanging effigies of Hirohito and Tojo from a makeshift gallows in front of City Hall.

"Other cars were dragging the emperor in the rear," Beane wrote, "and others just had stuffed images tied atop their mudguards, much as the proud sportsmen tote their deer southward from the New Hampshire woodlands in early winter."

Wily officials tried to curtail the carousing by immediately closing the liquor stores and private clubs, but as one reporter noted, "It's a difficult task to shut off beer or liquor supplies from determined Yanks, and some who had stocked up in advance were full of good cheer as a result."

At least one man was too full. Acting Police Chief Walter Guiney said the man "had been celebrating somewhat seriously and thinking he was at home, went to sleep on the Merrimack Common. This act in itself wasn't serious except that he was found by Officer Daniel Wade without any pants, shoes and stockings on. He said he could not remember how he got there."

At least he wasn't adding to the pedestrian congestion on Elm Street. Once regular police and the MPs were finally taxed to the max, County Attorney J. Vincent Broderick was abruptly drafted to direct traffic at Hanover and Elm.

Given the gridlock, it was an easy job.

Yes, to a working class city grown weary of war, it was time to celebrate. The only thing that was moving was the very scene itself.